# Introduction: A Prologue from the Bard

Brave scholars, blessed with time and energy,
    At school, fair Harvard, set about to glean,
From dusty tomes and modern poetry,
    All truths and knowledge formerly unseen.
From forth the hungry minds of these good folk
    Study guides, star-floss'd, soon came to life;
Whose deep and deft analysis awoke
    The latent "A"s of those in lit'rary strife.
Aim far past passing—insight from our trove
    Will free your comprehension from its cage.
Our SparkNotes' worth, online we also prove;
    Behold this book! Same brains, but paper page.
If patient or "whatever," please attend,
    What you have missed, our toil shall strive to mend.

# MUCH ADO ABOUT NOTHING

*William Shakespeare*

EDITORIAL DIRECTOR Justin Kestler
MANAGING EDITOR Ben Florman

SERIES EDITORS Boomie Aglietti, Justin Kestler
PRODUCTION Christian Lorentzen

WRITERS Miriam Jacobson, Susannah Mandel
EDITORS John Crowther, Benjamin Morgan

This edition published by Spark Publishing

Spark Publishing
A Division of SparkNotes LLC
120 Fifth Avenue, 8th Floor
New York, NY 10011

02 03 04 05 SN 9 8 7 6 5 4 3 2 1

Please send all comments and questions or report errors to
feedback@sparknotes.com.

Library of Congress information available upon request

Printed and bound in the United States

RRD-C

ISBN 1-58663-444-5

# CONTENTS

---

NOTE: This SparkNote refers to the text of *Much Ado About Nothing* given in *The Norton Shakespeare*, edited by Stephen Greenblatt. Other editions of the play may differ in line numbering, spelling, punctuation, and diction.

# CONTEXT

THE MOST INFLUENTIAL WRITER in all of English literature, William Shakespeare was born in 1564 to a successful middle-class glove-maker in Stratford-upon-Avon, England. Shakespeare attended grammar school, but his formal education proceeded no further. In 1582 he married an older woman, Anne Hathaway, and had three children with her. Around 1590 he left his family behind and traveled to London to work as an actor and playwright. Public and critical acclaim quickly followed, and Shakespeare eventually became the most popular playwright in England and part-owner of the Globe Theater. His career bridged the reigns of Elizabeth I (ruled 1558–1603) and James I (ruled 1603–1625), and he was a favorite of both monarchs. Indeed, James granted Shakespeare's company the greatest possible compliment by bestowing upon its members the title of King's Men. Wealthy and renowned, Shakespeare retired to Stratford and died in 1616 at the age of fifty-two. At the time of Shakespeare's death, literary luminaries such as Ben Jonson hailed his works as timeless.

Shakespeare's works were collected and printed in various editions in the century following his death, and by the early eighteenth century his reputation as the greatest poet ever to write in English was well established. The unprecedented admiration garnered by his works led to a fierce curiosity about Shakespeare's life, but the dearth of biographical information has left many details of Shakespeare's personal history shrouded in mystery. Some people have concluded from this fact and from Shakespeare's modest education that Shakespeare's plays were actually written by someone else—Francis Bacon and the Earl of Oxford are the two most popular candidates—but the support for this claim is overwhelmingly circumstantial, and the theory is not taken seriously by many scholars.

In the absence of credible evidence to the contrary, Shakespeare must be viewed as the author of the thirty-seven plays and 154 sonnets that bear his name. The legacy of this body of work is immense. A number of Shakespeare's plays seem to have transcended even the category of brilliance, becoming so influential as to affect profoundly the course of Western literature and culture ever after.

*Much Ado About Nothing* is generally considered one of Shakespeare's best comedies, because it combines elements of robust hilarity with more serious meditations on honor, shame, and court politics. It was probably written in 1598 and 1599, as Shakespeare was approaching the middle of his career. Like *As You Like It* and *Twelfth Night, Much Ado About Nothing,* though interspersed with darker concerns, is a joyful comedy that ends with multiple marriages and no deaths.

Although one of the features of Shakespearean comedy is that no one dies, it would be a mistake to assume that death is absent from this genre. Often, Shakespeare's comedies are more accepting of death than his tragedies, treating death as part of the natural cycle of life. *Much Ado About Nothing* is no exception, and Hero's pretending to die of humiliation makes death more vividly present here than in any of Shakespeare's other comedies. The crisis that lies at the center of *Much Ado About Nothing* troubles many readers and viewers, since the play creates a very strong sense of anger, betrayal, hatred, grief, and despair among the main characters. Although the crisis ends quickly, *Much Ado About Nothing* sometimes seems only steps away from becoming a tragedy.

Indeed, the line between tragedy and comedy is sometimes fuzzy. Many critics have noted that the plot of *Much Ado About Nothing* shares significant elements with that of *Romeo and Juliet. Much Ado About Nothing* also shares many features with Shakespeare's late play *The Winter's Tale,* which most critics assign to a different genre—that of problem comedy or romance. Like Hermione in *The Winter's Tale,* Hero stages a false death only to come back to life once her beloved has repented.

Although the young lovers Hero and Claudio provide the main impetus for the plot, the courtship between the older, wiser lovers Benedick and Beatrice is what makes *Much Ado About Nothing* so memorable. Benedick and Beatrice argue with delightful wit, and Shakespeare develops their journey from antagonism to sincere love and affection with a rich sense of humor and compassion. Since Beatrice and Benedick have a history behind them that adds weight to their relationship, they are older and more mature than the typical lovers in Shakespeare's comedies, though their unhealthy competitiveness reveals them to be childish novices when it comes to love.

# PLOT OVERVIEW

L EONATO, A KINDLY, RESPECTABLE NOBLEMAN, lives in the idyllic Italian town of Messina. Leonato shares his house with his lovely young daughter, Hero, his playful, clever niece, Beatrice, and his elderly brother, Antonio. As the play begins, Leonato prepares to welcome some friends home from a war. The friends include Don Pedro, a prince who is a close friend of Leonato, and two fellow soldiers: Claudio, a well-respected young nobleman, and Benedick, a clever man who constantly makes witty jokes, often at the expense of his friends. Don John, Don Pedro's illegitimate brother, is part of the crowd as well. Don John is sullen and bitter, and makes trouble for the others.

When the soldiers arrive at Leonato's home, Claudio quickly falls in love with Hero. Meanwhile, Benedick and Beatrice resume the war of witty insults that they have carried on with each other in the past. Claudio and Hero pledge their love to one another and decide to be married. To pass the time in the week before the wedding, the lovers and their friends decide to play a game. They want to get Beatrice and Benedick, who are clearly meant for each other, to stop arguing and fall in love. Their tricks prove successful, and Beatrice and Benedick soon fall secretly in love with each other.

But Don John has decided to disrupt everyone's happiness. He has his companion Borachio make love to Margaret, Hero's serving woman, at Hero's window in the darkness of the night, and he brings Don Pedro and Claudio to watch. Believing that he has seen Hero being unfaithful to him, the enraged Claudio humiliates Hero by suddenly accusing her of lechery on the day of their wedding and abandoning her at the altar. Hero's stricken family members decide to pretend that she died suddenly of shock and grief and to hide her away while they wait for the truth about her innocence to come to light. In the aftermath of the rejection, Benedick and Beatrice finally confess their love to one another. Fortunately, the night watchmen overhear Borachio bragging about his crime. Dogberry and Verges, the heads of the local police, ultimately arrest both Borachio and Conrad, another of Don John's followers. Everyone learns that Hero is really innocent, and Claudio, who believes she is dead, grieves for her.

Leonato tells Claudio that, as punishment, he wants Claudio to tell everybody in the city how innocent Hero was. He also wants Claudio to marry Leonato's "niece"—a girl who, he says, looks much like the dead Hero. Claudio goes to church with the others, preparing to marry the mysterious, masked woman he thinks is Hero's cousin. When Hero reveals herself as the masked woman, Claudio is overwhelmed with joy. Benedick then asks Beatrice if she will marry him, and after some arguing they agree. The joyful lovers all have a merry dance before they celebrate their double wedding.

# CHARACTER LIST

**Beatrice**   Leonato's niece and Hero's cousin. Beatrice is "a
pleasant-spirited lady" with a very sharp tongue. She is
generous and loving, but, like Benedick, continually
mocks other people with elaborately tooled jokes and
puns. She wages a war of wits against Benedick and
often wins the battles. At the outset of the play, she
appears content never to marry.

**Benedick**   An aristocratic soldier who has recently been fighting
under Don Pedro, and a friend of Don Pedro and
Claudio. Benedick is very witty, always making jokes
and puns. He carries on a "merry war" of wits with
Beatrice, but at the beginning of the play he swears he
will never fall in love or marry.

**Claudio**   A young soldier who has won great acclaim fighting
under Don Pedro during the recent wars. Claudio falls
in love with Hero upon his return to Messina. His
unfortunately suspicious nature makes him quick to
believe evil rumors and hasty to despair and
take revenge.

**Hero**   The beautiful young daughter of Leonato and the
cousin of Beatrice. Hero is lovely, gentle, and kind. She
falls in love with Claudio when he falls for her, but
when Don John slanders her and Claudio rashly takes
revenge, she suffers terribly.

**Don Pedro**   An important nobleman from Aragon, sometimes
referred to as "Prince." Don Pedro is a longtime friend
of Leonato, Hero's father, and is also close to the
soldiers who have been fighting under him—the
younger Benedick and the very young Claudio. Don
Pedro is generous, courteous, intelligent, and loving to
his friends, but he is also quick to believe evil of others
and hasty to take revenge. He is the most politically
and socially powerful character in the play.

*Leonato*   A respected, well-to-do, elderly noble at whose home, in Messina, Italy, the action is set. Leonato is the father of Hero and the uncle of Beatrice. As governor of Messina, he is second in social power only to Don Pedro.

*Don John*   The illegitimate brother of Don Pedro; sometimes called "the Bastard." Don John is melancholy and sullen by nature, and he creates a dark scheme to ruin the happiness of Hero and Claudio. He is the villain of the play; his evil actions are motivated by his envy of his brother's social authority.

*Margaret*   Hero's serving woman, who unwittingly helps Borachio and Don John deceive Claudio into thinking that Hero is unfaithful. Unlike Ursula, Hero's other lady-in-waiting, Margaret is lower class. Though she is honest, she does have some dealings with the villainous world of Don John: her lover is the mistrustful and easily bribed Borachio. Also unlike Ursula, Margaret loves to break decorum, especially with bawdy jokes and teases.

*Borachio*   An associate of Don John. Borachio is the lover of Margaret, Hero's serving woman. He conspires with Don John to trick Claudio and Don Pedro into thinking that Hero is unfaithful to Claudio. His name means "drunkard" in Italian, which might serve as a subtle direction to the actor playing him.

*Conrad*   One of Don John's more intimate associates, entirely devoted to Don John. Several recent productions have staged Conrad as Don John's potential male lover, possibly to intensify Don John's feelings of being a social outcast and therefore motivate his desire for revenge.

*Dogberry*   The constable in charge of the Watch, or chief policeman, of Messina. Dogberry is very sincere and takes his job seriously, but he has a habit of using exactly the wrong word to convey his meaning.

Dogberry is one of the few "middling sort," or middle-class characters, in the play, though his desire to speak formally and elaborately like the noblemen becomes an occasion for parody.

*Verges*   The deputy to Dogberry, chief policeman of Messina.

*Antonio*   Leonato's elderly brother, and Hero and Beatrice's uncle.

*Balthasar*   A waiting man in Leonato's household and a musician. Balthasar flirts with Margaret at the masked party and helps Leonato, Claudio, and Don Pedro trick Benedick into falling in love with Beatrice. Balthasar sings the song, "Sigh no more, ladies, sigh no more" about accepting men's infidelity as natural.

*Ursula*   One of Hero's waiting women.

CHARACTER LIST

# ANALYSIS OF MAJOR CHARACTERS

## BEATRICE

Beatrice is the niece of Leonato, a wealthy governor of Messina. Though she is close friends with her cousin Hero, Leonato's daughter, the two could not be less alike. Whereas Hero is polite, quiet, respectful, and gentle, Beatrice is feisty, cynical, witty, and sharp. Beatrice keeps up a "merry war" of wits with Benedick, a lord and soldier from Padua. The play suggests that she was once in love with Benedick but that he led her on and their relationship ended. Now when they meet, the two constantly compete to outdo one another with clever insults.

Although she appears hardened and sharp, Beatrice is really vulnerable. Once she overhears Hero describing that Benedick is in love with her (Beatrice), she opens herself to the sensitivities and weaknesses of love. Beatrice is a prime example of one of Shakespeare's strong female characters. She refuses to marry because she has not discovered the perfect, equal partner and because she is unwilling to eschew her liberty and submit to the will of a controlling husband. When Hero has been humiliated and accused of violating her chastity, Beatrice explodes with fury at Claudio for mistreating her cousin. In her frustration and rage about Hero's mistreatment, Beatrice rebels against the unequal status of women in Renaissance society. "O that I were a man for his sake! Or that I had any friend would be a man for my sake!" she passionately exclaims. "I cannot be a man with wishing, therefore I will die a woman with grieving" (IV.i.312–318).

## BENEDICK

Benedick is the willful lord, recently returned from fighting in the wars, who vows that he will never marry. He engages with Beatrice in a competition to outwit, outsmart, and out-insult the other, but to his observant friends, he seems to feel some deeper emotion below the surface. Upon hearing Claudio and Don Pedro discussing

Beatrice's desire for him, Benedick vows to be "horribly in love with her," in effect continuing the competition by outdoing her in love and courtship (II.iii.207). Benedick is one of the most histrionic characters in the play, as he constantly performs for the benefit of others. He is the entertainer, indulging in witty hyperbole to express his feelings. He delivers a perfect example of his inflated rhetoric when Beatrice enters during the masked ball. Turning to his companions, Benedick grossly exaggerates how Beatrice has misused him, bidding his friends to send him to the farthest corners of the earth rather than let him spend one more minute with his nemesis: "Will your grace command me any service to the world's end? I will go on the slightest errand now to the Antipodes that you can devise to send me on. I will fetch you a toothpicker from the furthest inch of Asia . . . do you any embassage to the pigmies, rather than hold three words' conference with this harpy" (II.i.229–235).

Of course, since Benedick is so invested in performing for the others, it is not easy for us to tell whether he has been in love with Beatrice all along or falls in love with her suddenly during the play. Benedick's adamant refusal to marry does appear to change over the course of the play, once he decides to fall in love with Beatrice. He attempts to conceal this transformation from his friends but really might enjoy shocking them by shaving off his beard and professing undying love to Beatrice. This change in attitude seems most evident when Benedick challenges Claudio, previously his closest friend in the world, to duel to the death over Claudio's accusation as to Hero's unchaste behavior. There can be no doubt at this point that Benedick has switched his allegiances entirely over to Beatrice.

## DON PEDRO, PRINCE OF ARAGON

Of all the main characters in *Much Ado About Nothing,* Don Pedro seems the most elusive. He is the noblest character in the social hierarchy of the play, and his friends Benedick and Claudio, though equals in wit, must always defer to him because their positions depend upon his favor. Don Pedro has power, and he is well aware of it; whether or not he abuses this power is open to question. Unlike his bastard brother, the villain Don John, Don Pedro most often uses his power and authority toward positive ends. But like his half-brother, Don Pedro manipulates other characters as much as he likes. For instance, he insists on wooing Hero for Claudio himself, while masked, rather than allowing Claudio to profess his love to

Hero first. Of course, everything turns out for the best—Don Pedro's motives are purely in the interest of his friend. But we are left wondering why Don Pedro feels the need for such an elaborate dissimulation merely to inform Hero of Claudio's romantic interest. It seems simply that it is Don Pedro's royal prerogative to do exactly as he wishes, and no one can question it. Despite his cloudy motives, Don Pedro does work to bring about happiness. It is his idea, for instance, to convince Beatrice and Benedick that each is in love with the other and by doing so bring the two competitors together. He orchestrates the whole plot and plays the role of director in this comedy of wit and manners.

Don Pedro is the only one of the three gallants not to end up with a wife at the end. Benedick laughingly jokes in the final scene that the melancholy prince must "get thee a wife" in order to enjoy true happiness (V.iv.117). The question necessarily arises as to why Don Pedro is sad at the end of a joyous comedy. Perhaps his exchange with Beatrice at the masked ball—in which he proposes marriage to her and she jokingly refuses him, taking his proposal as mere sport—pains him; perhaps he is truly in love with Beatrice. The text does not give us a conclusive explanation for his melancholy, nor for his fascination with dissembling. This uncertainly about his character helps to make him one of the most thought-provoking characters in the play.

# THEMES, MOTIFS & SYMBOLS

## THEMES

*Themes are the fundamental and often universal ideas explored in a literary work.*

### THE IDEAL OF SOCIAL GRACE

The characters' dense, colorful manner of speaking represents the ideal that Renaissance courtiers strove for in their social interactions. The play's language is heavily laden with metaphor and ornamented by rhetoric. Benedick, Claudio, and Don Pedro all produce the kind of witty banter that courtiers used to attract attention and approval in noble households. Courtiers were expected to speak in highly contrived language but to make their clever performances seem effortless. The most famous model for this kind of behavior is Baldassare Castiglione's sixteenth-century manual *The Courtier,* translated into English by Thomas Hoby in 1561. According to this work, the ideal courtier masks his effort and appears to project elegance and natural grace by means of what Castiglione calls *sprezzatura,* the illusion of effortlessness. Benedick and his companions try to display their polished social graces both in their behavior and in their speech.

The play pokes fun at the fanciful language of love that courtiers used. When Claudio falls in love, he tries to be the perfect courtier by using intricate language. As Benedick notes: "His words are a very fantastical banquet, just so many strange dishes" (II.iii.18–19). Although the young gallants in the play seem casual in their displays of wit, they constantly struggle to maintain their social positions. Benedick and Claudio must constantly strive to remain in Don Pedro's favor. When Claudio silently agrees to let Don Pedro take his place to woo Hero, it is quite possible that he does so not because he is too shy to woo the woman himself, but because he must accede to Don Pedro's authority in order to stay in Don Pedro's good favor. When Claudio believes that Don Pedro has deceived him and wooed Hero not for Claudio but for himself, he cannot drop his polite civility, even though he is full of despair. Beatrice jokes that Claudio is "civil as an orange," punning on the Seville orange, a bitter fruit (II.i.256). Claudio remains polite and nearly silent even though he is upset, telling Benedick of Don Pedro and Hero: "I wish him joy of her" (II.i.170). Clearly, Claudio chooses his obedience to Don Pedro over his love for Hero.

Claudio displays social grace, but his strict adherence to social propriety eventually leads him into a trap. He abandons Hero at the wedding because Don John leads him to believe that she is unchaste (marriage to an unchaste woman would be socially unacceptable). But Don John's plan to unseat Claudio does not succeed, of course, as Claudio remains Don Pedro's favorite, and it is Hero who has to suffer until her good reputation is restored.

### DECEPTION AS A MEANS TO AN END

The plot of *Much Ado About Nothing* is based upon deliberate deceptions, some malevolent and others benign. The duping of Claudio and Don Pedro results in Hero's disgrace, while the ruse of her death prepares the way for her redemption and reconciliation with Claudio. In a more lighthearted vein, Beatrice and Benedick are fooled into thinking that each loves the other, and they actually do fall in love as a result. *Much Ado About Nothing* shows that deceit is not inherently evil, but something that can be used as a means to good or bad ends.

In the play, it is sometimes difficult to distinguish between good and bad deception. When Claudio announces his desire to woo Hero, Don Pedro takes it upon himself to woo her for Claudio. Then, at the instigation of Don John, Claudio begins to mistrust Don Pedro, thinking he has been deceived. Just as the play's audience comes to believe, temporarily, in the illusions of the theater, so the play's characters become caught up in the illusions that they help to create for one another. Benedick and Beatrice flirt caustically at the masked ball, each possibly aware of the other's presence yet pretending not to know the person hiding behind the mask. Likewise, when Claudio has shamed and rejected Hero, Leonato and his household "publish" that Hero has died in order to punish Claudio for his mistake. When Claudio returns, penitent, to accept the hand of Leonato's "niece" (actually Hero), a group of masked women enters and Claudio must wed blindly. The masking of Hero and the other women reveals that the social institution of marriage has little to do with love. When Claudio flounders and asks, "Which is the lady I must seize upon?" he is ready and willing to commit the rest of his life to one of a group of unknowns (V.iv.53). His willingness stems not only from his guilt about slandering an innocent woman but also from the fact that he may care more about rising in Leonato's favor than in marrying for love. In the end, deceit is neither purely positive nor purely negative: it is a means to an end, a way to create an illusion that helps one succeed socially.

### THE IMPORTANCE OF HONOR

The aborted wedding ceremony, in which Claudio rejects Hero, accusing her of infidelity and violated chastity and publicly shaming her in front of her father, is the climax of the play. In Shakespeare's time, a woman's honor was based upon her virginity and chaste behavior. For a woman to lose her honor by having sexual relations before marriage meant that she would lose all social standing, a disaster from which she could never recover. Moreover, this loss of honor would poison the woman's whole family. Thus, when Leonato rashly believes Claudio's shaming of Hero at the wedding ceremony, he tries to obliterate her entirely: "Hence from her, let her die" (IV.i.153). Furthermore, he speaks of her loss of honor as an indelible stain from which he cannot distance himself, no matter how hard he tries: "O she is fallen / Into a pit of ink, that the wide sea / Hath drops too few to wash her clean again" (IV.i.138–140). For women in that era, the loss of honor was a form of annihilation.

For men, on the other hand, honor depended on male friendship alliances and was more military in nature. Unlike a woman, a man could defend his honor, and that of his family, by fighting in a battle or a duel. Beatrice urges Benedick to avenge Hero's honor by dueling to the death with Claudio. As a woman, Hero cannot seize back her honor, but Benedick can do it for her via physical combat.

## MOTIFS

*Motifs are recurring structures, contrasts, or literary devices that can help to develop and inform the text's major themes.*

### PUBLIC SHAMING

Even though Hero is ultimately vindicated, her public shaming at the wedding ceremony is too terrible to be ignored. In a sense, this kind of humiliation incurs more damage to her honor and her family name than would an act of unchaste behavior—an transgression she never commits. The language that both Claudio and Leonato use to shame Hero is extremely strong. To Claudio she is a "rotten orange" (IV.i.30), and to Leonato a rotting carcass that cannot be preserved: "the wide sea / Hath ... / ... salt too little which may season give / To her foul tainted flesh!" (IV.i.139–142).

Shame is also what Don John hopes will cause Claudio to lose his place as Don Pedro's favorite: once Claudio is discovered to be engaged to a loose woman, Don John believes that Don Pedro will reject Claudio as he rejected Don John long ago. Shame is a form of social punishment closely connected to loss of honor. A product of an illegitimate sexual coupling himself, Don John has grown up constantly reminded of his own social shame, and he will do anything to right the balance. Ironically, in the end Don John is shamed and threatened with torture to punish him for deceiving the company. Clearly, he will never gain a good place in courtly society.

NOTING

In Shakespeare's time, the "Nothing" of the title would have been pronounced "Noting." Thus, the play's title could read: "Much Ado About Noting." Indeed, many of the players participate in the actions of observing, listening, and writing, or noting. In order for a plot hinged on instances of deceit to work, the characters must note one another constantly. When the women manipulate Beatrice into believing that Benedick adores her, they conceal themselves in the orchard so that Beatrice can better note their conversation. Since they know that Beatrice loves to eavesdrop, they are sure that their plot will succeed: "look where Beatrice like a lapwing runs / Close by the ground to hear our conference," notes Hero (III.i.24–25). Each line the women speak is a carefully placed note for Beatrice to take up and ponder; the same is true of the scheme to convince Benedick of Beatrice's passion.

Don John's plot to undo Claudio also hinges on noting: in order for Claudio to believe that Hero is unchaste and unfaithful, he must be brought to her window to witness, or note, Margaret (whom he takes to be Hero) bidding farewell to Borachio in the semidarkness. Dogberry, Verges, and the rest of the comical night watch discover and arrest Don John because, although ill-equipped to express themselves linguistically, they overhear talk of the Margaret-Borachio staging. Despite their verbal deficiencies, they manage to capture Don John and bring him to Leonato, after having had the sexton (a church official) "note" the occurrences of the evening in writing. In the end, noting, in the sense of writing, unites Beatrice and Benedick for good: Hero and Claudio reveal love sonnets written by Beatrice and Benedick, textual evidence that notes and proves their love for one another.

### ENTERTAINMENT

From the witty yet plaintive song that Balthasar sings about the deceitfulness of men to the masked ball and the music and dancing at the end of the play, the characters of *Much Ado About Nothing* spend much of their time engaging in elaborate spectacles and entertainments. The play's title encapsulates the sentiment of effervescent and light court entertainment: the two hours' traffic onstage will be entertaining, comic, and absorbing. The characters who merrily spar and fall in love in the beginning will, of course, end up together in the conclusion. Beatrice compares courtship and marriage to delightful court dances: "wooing, wedding and repenting is as a Scotch jig, a measure, and a cinquepace" (II.i.60–61). By including a masquerade as court entertainment in the middle, as well as two songs and a dance at the end, the play presents itself as sheer entertainment, conscious of its own theatricality.

### COUNTERFEITING

The idea of counterfeiting, in the sense of presenting a false face to the world, appears frequently throughout the play. A particularly rich and complex example of counterfeiting occurs as Leonato, Claudio, and Don Pedro pretend that Beatrice is head over heels in love with Benedick so that the eavesdropping Benedick will overhear it and believe it. Luring Benedick into this trap, Leonato ironically dismisses the idea that perhaps Beatrice counterfeits her desire for Benedick, as he and the others counterfeit this love themselves: "O God! Counterfeit? There was never counterfeit of passion came so near the life of passion as she discovers it" (II.iii.98–99).

Another, more serious reference to counterfeiting occurs at the wedding ceremony, as Claudio rhetorically paints a picture of Hero as a perfect counterfeit of innocence, unchaste and impure beneath a seemingly unblemished surface:

> She's but the sign and semblance of her honour.
> Behold how like a maid she blushes here!
> O, what authority and show of truth
> Can cunning sin cover itself withal!
>
> (IV.i.31–34)

Hero's supposed counterfeiting is of a grave nature, as it threatens her womanly reputation. It is not her emotions that are being misconstrued, as with Beatrice, but rather her character and integrity.

## SYMBOLS

*Symbols are objects, characters, figures, or colors used to represent abstract ideas or concepts.*

### THE TAMING OF WILD ANIMALS

The play is peppered with metaphors involving the taming of wild animals. In the case of the courtship between Beatrice and Benedick, the symbol of a tamed savage animal represents the social taming that must occur for both wild souls to be ready to submit themselves to the shackles of love and marriage. Beatrice's vow to submit to Benedick's love by "[t]aming my wild heart to thy loving hand" makes use of terms from falconry, suggesting that Benedick is to become Beatrice's master (III.i.113). In the opening act, Claudio and Don Pedro tease Benedick about his aversion to marriage, comparing him to a wild animal. Don Pedro quotes a common adage, "'In time the savage bull doth bear the yoke,'" meaning that in time even the savage Benedick will surrender to the taming of love and marriage (I.i.213). Benedick mocks this sentiment, professing that he will never submit to the will of a woman. At the very end, when Benedick and Beatrice agree to marry, Claudio pokes fun at Benedick's mortified countenance, suggesting that Benedick is reluctant to marry because he remembers the allusion to tamed bulls:

> Tush, fear not, man, we'll tip thy horns with gold,
> And all Europa shall rejoice at thee
> As once Europa did at lusty Jove
> When he would play the noble beast in love.
> (V.iv.44–47)

Claudio changes Benedick from a laboring farm animal, a bull straining under a yoke, to a wild god, empowered by his bestial form to take sexual possession of his lady. While the bull of marriage is the sadly yoked, formerly savage creature, the bull that Claudio refers to comes from the classical myth in which Zeus took the form of a bull and carried off the mortal woman Europa. This second bull is supposed to represent the other side of the coin: the bull of bestial male sexuality.

## WAR

Throughout the play, images of war frequently symbolize verbal arguments and confrontations. At the beginning of the play, Leonato relates to the other characters that there is a "merry war" between Beatrice and Benedick: "They never meet but there's a skirmish of wit between them" (I.i.50–51). Beatrice carries on this martial imagery, describing how, when she won the last duel with Benedick, "four of his five wits went halting off" (I.i.53). When Benedick arrives, their witty exchange resembles the blows and parries of a well-executed fencing match. Leonato accuses Claudio of killing Hero with words: "Thy slander hath gone through and through her heart" (V.i.68). Later in the same scene, Benedick presents Claudio with a violent verbal challenge: to duel to the death over Hero's honor. When Borachio confesses to staging the loss of Hero's innocence, Don Pedro describes this spoken evidence as a sword that tears through Claudio's heart: "Runs not this speech like iron through your blood?" (V.i.227), and Claudio responds that he has already figuratively committed suicide upon hearing these words: "I have drunk poison whiles he uttered it" (V.i.228).

## HERO'S DEATH

Claudio's powerful words accusing Hero of unchaste and disloyal acts cause her to fall down in apparent lifelessness. Leonato accentuates the direness of Hero's state, pushing her further into seeming death by renouncing her, "Hence from her, let her die" (IV.i.153). When Friar Francis, Hero, and Beatrice convince Leonato of his daughter's innocence, they maintain that she really has died, in order to punish Claudio and give Hero a respectable amount of time to regain her honor, which, although not lost, has been publicly savaged. Claudio performs all the actions of mourning Hero, paying a choir to sing a dirge at her tomb. In a symbolic sense, Hero has died, since, although she is pure, Claudio's damning accusation has permanently besmirched her name. She must symbolically die and be reborn pure again in order for Claudio to marry her a second time. Hero's false death is less a charade aimed to induce remorse in Claudio than it is a social ritual designed to cleanse her name and person of infamy.

# SUMMARY & ANALYSIS

## ACT I, SCENE I

*[A]nd in such great letters as they write "Here is good
horse to hire" let them signify under my sign "Here
you may see Benedick, the married man."*

(See QUOTATIONS, p. 51)

SUMMARY

In the Italian town of Messina, the wealthy and kindly Leonato prepares to welcome home some soldier friends who are returning from
a battle. These friends include Don Pedro of Aragon, a highly
respected nobleman, and a brave young soldier named Claudio,
who has won much honor in the fighting. Leonato's young daughter, Hero, and her cousin, Beatrice, accompany him. Beatrice asks
about the health of another soldier in Don Pedro's army, a man
named Signor Benedick. Beatrice cleverly mocks and insults Benedick. A messenger from Don Pedro defends Benedick as an honor-
able and virtuous man, but Leonato explains that Beatrice and
Benedick carry on a "merry war" of wits with one another, trading
jibes whenever they meet. Beatrice confirms this statement, noting
that in their most recent conflict, "four of his five wits went halting
off, and now is the whole man governed with one" (I.i.52–54).

Don Pedro arrives at Leonato's house with his two friends, Claudio and Benedick, and they are joyfully welcomed. Also accompa-
nying Don Pedro is his quiet, sullen, illegitimate brother, Don John
"the Bastard," with whom Don Pedro has recently become friendly
after a period of mutual hostility. While Leonato and Don Pedro
have a private talk, Beatrice and Benedick take up their war of wits.
In an extremely fast-paced exchange of barbs, they insult one
another's looks, intelligence, and personality. When Benedick tells
Beatrice proudly that he has never loved a woman and never will,
Beatrice responds that women everywhere ought to rejoice.

Don Pedro tells Benedick, Claudio, and Don John that Leonato
has invited them all to stay with him for a month, and that Don
Pedro has accepted. Everyone goes off together except Claudio and
Benedick. Claudio shyly asks Benedick what he thinks of Hero,

announcing that he has fallen in love with her. Benedick jokingly plays down Hero's beauty, teasing Claudio for thinking about becoming a tame husband. But when Don Pedro returns to look for his friends, Benedick tells him Claudio's secret, and Don Pedro approves highly of the match. Since Claudio is shy and Leonato is Don Pedro's close friend, Don Pedro proposes a trick: at the costume ball to be held that night, Don Pedro will disguise himself as Claudio and declare his love to Hero. He will then talk with Leonato, her father, which should enable Claudio to win Hero without difficulty. Full of plans and excitement, the three friends head off to get ready for the ball.

### ANALYSIS: ACT I, SCENE 1

This opening scene introduces all of the major characters, as well as the play's setting—Leonato's welcoming, friendly house in Messina. Don Pedro and the others are just returning from a war in which they have been victorious, seemingly setting the stage for a relaxed, happy comedy in which the main characters fall in love and have fun together. While the play opens with a strong feeling of joy and calm, the harmony of Messina is certainly to be disturbed later on.

Beatrice and Benedick are perhaps Shakespeare's most famously witty characters; neither ever lets the other say anything without countering it with a pun or criticism. One notable characteristic of their attacks upon each other is their ability to extend a metaphor throughout lines of dialogue. When Benedick calls Beatrice a "rare parrot-teacher," Beatrice responds, "A bird of my tongue is better than a beast of yours" (I.i.114). Benedick continues the reference to animals in his response, saying, "I would my horse had the speed of your tongue" (I.i.115). It is as if each anticipates the other's response. Though their insults are biting, their ability to maintain such clever, interconnected sparring seems to illustrate the existence of a strong bond between them.

Beatrice and Benedick have courted in the past, and Beatrice's viciousness stems from the fact that Benedick previously abandoned her. When she insists that Benedick "set up his bills here in Messina and challenged Cupid at the flight, and my uncle's fool, reading the challenge, subscribed for Cupid," she describes a "battle" of love between herself and Benedick that she has lost (I.i.32–34). The result is what Leonato describes as "a kind of merry war betwixt Sir Benedick and [Beatrice]. They never meet but there's a skirmish of wit between them" (I.i.49–51).

Another purpose of the dialogue between Benedick and Beatrice, as well as that among Benedick, Claudio, and Don Pedro, is to explore the complex relationships between men and women. Both Benedick and Beatrice claim to scorn love. As Benedick says to Beatrice, "[I]t is certain I am loved of all ladies, only you excepted. And I would I could find it in my heart that I had not a hard heart, for truly I love none" (I.i.101–104). Benedick thus sets himself up as an unattainable object of desire. With her mocking reply that "I had rather hear my dog bark at a crow than a man swear he loves me," Beatrice similarly puts herself out of reach (I.i.107–108). Both at this point appear certain that they will never fall in love or marry.

Benedick's disdain for matrimony arises again when he realizes that Claudio is seriously contemplating asking Hero for her hand in marriage. Until this point, all the soldiers have exhibited a kind of macho pride in being bachelors, but Claudio now seems happy to find himself falling in love, and Don Pedro rejoices in his young friend's decision. Benedick alone swears, "I will live a bachelor" (I.i.201). Don Pedro's teasing rejoinder, "I shall see thee ere I die look pale with love. . . . 'In time the savage bull doth bear the yoke,' " suggests his belief that love does conquer all, even those as stubborn as Benedick (I.i.202–214).

## ACT I, SCENES II–III

### SUMMARY: ACT I, SCENE II
Inside his house, Leonato runs into his elder brother, Antonio. Antonio says that a servant of his overheard Don Pedro talking with Claudio outside. The servant thinks that he overheard Don Pedro professing his love for Hero and that he means to tell her that very night, during the dance, and then ask Leonato himself for Hero's hand in marriage. Obviously, Antonio has misheard the truth: Claudio, not Don Pedro, loves Hero. Nevertheless, the only part of the conversation Antonio has intercepted is that Don Pedro will woo Hero that evening. Leonato's prudent reply is that he will not consider the rumor to be true until his daughter is actually courted. But he declares that he will tell Hero about it, so that she may think about what she wants to say in response to Don Pedro, should this bit of information prove true.

## SUMMARY: ACT I, SCENE III

Elsewhere in the house, Don John converses with his servant, Conrad. Conrad asks Don John why he appears angry and melancholy. Don John replies that he is naturally depressed and somber; he lacks the skills—or the willpower—to change his face to suit other people. Conrad reminds Don John that Don Pedro has only very recently started to be friendly with him again, and if Don John wants to remain on good terms with his powerful brother, he ought to show a more cheerful face. But, bitter that he must depend both socially and economically on his much more successful and highly ranked brother, Don John bristles at having to conform to Don Pedro's expectations.

Borachio, another of Don John's servants, enters to tell Don John that he has overheard rumors of the upcoming marriage between Claudio and Hero. Borachio, like Leonato's servant, has also overheard Don Pedro and Claudio making plans, but Borachio correctly understands what he has heard. He realizes that Don Pedro plans to court Hero in order to give her to Claudio. Don John, who hates Claudio for being so well loved and respected, decides to try to use this information to make trouble for Claudio. Conrad and Borachio swear to help him.

---

## ANALYSIS: ACT I, SCENES II–III

Overhearing, plotting, and misunderstanding occur frequently in *Much Ado About Nothing,* as characters constantly eavesdrop or spy on other characters. Occasionally they learn the truth, but more often they misunderstand what they see or hear, or they are tricked into believing what other people want them to believe. In these scenes, Antonio's servant and Don John's associate both overhear the same conversation between Don Pedro and Claudio, but only Borachio understands it correctly, while Antonio's servant (and, consequently, Antonio himself) misunderstand. He carries this incorrect information onward, first to Leonato and then to Hero.

It appears that Don John has no strong motive for the villainy he commits and that his actions are inspired by a bad nature, something he acknowledges fully: "though I cannot be said to be a flattering honest man, it must not be denied but I am a plain-dealing villain" (I.iii.23–25). Yet, the fact that Don John is Don Pedro's bastard brother—that he is of a much lower station than Don Pedro and possesses little chance of rising in society because of his bastard birth—suggests that there is more to his behavior than his evil character. He most likely resents Don Pedro, the most powerful figure in the play's social hierarchy, for claiming the authority and social superiority of a legitimate heir. His jealousy of his brother's success is most likely what drives him to wreak havoc on Claudio and Don Pedro. His insistence on honesty in this scene might appear admirable, but he lies to many people later on, casting his statements here about being harmless into doubt.

To understand Don John's claim of natural evil, we should remember that he stands in a very difficult position. As the illegitimate brother (or half-brother) of Don Pedro, Don John is labeled "the Bastard." Illegitimate sons of noblemen found themselves in a tricky position in Renaissance England. Often, their fathers acknowledged them and gave them money and an education, but they could never be their fathers' real heirs, and they were often excluded from polite society and looked upon with disdain. In plays, bastard sons were sometimes admired for their individualism, enterprise, and courage, but in Shakespeare's works, their anger about their unfair exclusion often inspires them to villainy. Like Edmund in Shakespeare's tragedy *King Lear,* Don John seems to be a villain at least in part because he is a bastard, and like Edmund he is determined to cross his legitimate brother in any way that he can.

In *Much Ado About Nothing,* Don John is in the difficult position of having to behave well and court favor with his more powerful brother, Don Pedro, while at the same time being excluded from the privileges Don Pedro enjoys because of his illegitimacy. Don John is bitter about the restrictions imposed upon him: "I am trusted with a muzzle, and enfranchised with a clog. Therefore I have decreed not to sing in my cage" (I.iii.25–27). He complains, in essence, that he is not trusted at all and not given any freedom; he rails against the constraints of his role, refusing to "sing" in his "cage," or make the best of things. Instead, he seems to want to take out his frustrations by manipulating and hurting other people for his own amusement. Don John's claim that he hates Claudio because he is jealous of Claudio's friendship with his brother seems questionable; it seems more likely that Don John simply hates anyone happy and well liked and thus wants to exact a more general revenge upon the world.

## ACT II, SCENE I

*[H]e that is more than a youth is not for me, and he*
*that is less than a man, I am not for him.*

(See QUOTATIONS, p. 52)

### SUMMARY

While Hero, Beatrice, Leonato, and Antonio wait for the evening's masked ball to begin, Hero and Beatrice discuss their idea of the perfect man—a happy medium between Don John, who never talks, and Benedick, who engages himself in constant banter. This exchange leads into a conversation about whether or not Beatrice will ever get a husband, and Beatrice laughingly claims that she will not. Leonato and Antonio also remind Hero about their belief that Don Pedro plans to propose to her that evening. The other partygoers enter, and the men put on masks. Supposedly, the women now cannot tell who the men are. The music begins, and the dancers pair off and hold conversations while they dance. Don Pedro's musician, Balthasar, dances with Hero's servant Margaret and old Antonio dances with Hero's other servant, Ursula. Meanwhile, Don Pedro dances with Hero and begins to flirt with her. Benedick dances with Beatrice, who either does not recognize him or pretends not to. She insults Benedick thoroughly to her dancing partner, saying that while Benedick thinks that he is witty others find him completely boring.

The music leads many of the dancers away into corners of the stage, creating various couplings. Don John, who has seen his brother Don Pedro courting Hero, decides to make Claudio jealous by making him think that Don Pedro has decided to win and keep Hero for himself instead of giving her to Claudio as he had promised. Pretending not to recognize Claudio behind his mask, Don John addresses him as if he were Benedick, mentioning to him that, contrary to their plan, Don Pedro actually courts Hero for himself and means to marry her that very night.

Claudio believes Don John, and, when the real Benedick enters a few moments later, the angry and miserable Claudio rushes out. But when Don Pedro comes in along with Hero and Leonato, Benedick learns that Don Pedro has been true to his word after all; he has courted and won Hero for Claudio, not for himself, just as he promised. Benedick still remains bitter about the nasty things Beatrice said to him during the dance, so when Beatrice approaches with

Claudio, he begs Don Pedro to send him on some extremely arduous errand rather than be forced to endure her company. Don Pedro laughingly insists that he stay, but Benedick leaves anyway.

When Claudio returns, Don Pedro tells him that Hero has agreed to marry him (Claudio), and Leonato supports him. Claudio, overwhelmed, can barely speak, but he and Hero privately make their promises to one another. Beatrice half-seriously remarks that she will never have a husband, and Don Pedro offers himself to her. Beatrice, comparing him to fancy clothes, replies that she wishes she could have him but that he would be too lavish and valuable for her to wear every day. After Beatrice and Benedick leave, Leonato and Claudio discuss when Claudio will marry Hero. Claudio wants the wedding to occur the next day, but Leonato decides on the coming Monday, only a week away. Claudio regrets that the wait will be so long, but Don Pedro comes up with a good way to pass the time: with the help of all his friends, he will design a plan to get Beatrice and Benedick to stop arguing and fall in love with one another. He secures the promises of Leonato, Claudio, and Hero to help him in the plan he will devise.

### ANALYSIS

This long scene resolves the first of the play's important questions: whether Claudio will receive Hero's consent to love and marry her. When the two lovers are finally brought together, Claudio is too overwhelmed with joy to profess his love in elevated language, saying to Hero simply, "Silence is the perfectest herald of joy. I were but little happy if I could say how much" (II.i.267–268). While Claudio can find few words to express his joy, Hero can find none. Indeed, it is Beatrice who formalizes Hero's return of Claudio's love, commenting to Claudio, "My cousin [Hero] tells him [Claudio] in his ear that he is in her heart" (II.i.275–276). We never hear Hero's acceptance of Claudio, but nonetheless we know what occurs.

These two quiet characters—Claudio and Hero—seem well matched, and Claudio's addressing of Beatrice as "cousin" confirms that he will soon marry into her family (II.i.277). Nonetheless, a troubling element of Claudio's character comes to light in this scene. Don John's attempt to thwart the match has come to nothing; although he does manage to trick Claudio into believing that Don Pedro has betrayed him and is going to marry Hero himself, Claudio learns the truth before anything bad can happen. But here we see that Claudio is prone to making rash decisions. He is very quick to believe that his friend has betrayed him, not even questioning Don John's claims. Acknowledging that Don Pedro seems to be wooing Hero for himself, Claudio declares that

> Friendship is constant . . .
> Save in the office and affairs of love.
> . . .
> . . . Farewell, therefore, Hero.
>
> (II.i.153–160)

Claudio's readiness to believe that his friend would betray him is disturbing, and Don John's plotting coupled with Claudio's gullibility ominously foreshadows worse things to follow.

Beatrice and Benedick continue their "merry war" of wits with one another, but it seems to veer off course and turn into a much more hurtful competition. This time, Beatrice gets the better of Benedick while Benedick cannot defend himself. Dancing with him during the ball, while masked, she insults Benedick by mocking his "wittiness" and declaring his jokes boring. Beatrice's jabs at Benedick are psychologically astute. We see how apt her comments are when Benedick cannot stop repeating her words to himself later in the scene. Moreover, the fact that Benedick begs Don Pedro frantically to let him leave so he will not have to talk to Beatrice suggests that he finds her company not simply annoying but also damaging.

Though Beatrice repeats in this scene her intention never to marry, her attitude seems a little changed. A certain wistfulness marks her words as she watches the betrothal of Hero to Claudio: "Good Lord, for alliance! There goes everyone to the world but I, and I am sunburnt. I may sit in a corner and cry 'Heigh-ho for a husband!'" (II.i.278–280). Beatrice jests, as always, but it is hard to tell how seriously she takes this matter. Don Pedro's sudden offer of himself to her in marriage also seems both lighthearted and serious, and Beatrice's gentle rejection of him compels us to wonder whether she really does want to get married.

# ACT II, SCENES II–III

> *By my troth it is no addition to her wit—nor no great*
> *argument of her folly, for I will be horribly in love*
> *with her.* (See QUOTATIONS, p. 53)

## SUMMARY: ACT II, SCENE II

The bitter and wicked Don John has learned of the upcoming marriage of Claudio and Hero, and he wishes that he could find a way to prevent it. Don John's servant Borachio devises a plan. Borachio is currently the lover of one of Hero's serving women, Margaret. He suggests that Don John go to Claudio and Don Pedro and tell them that Hero is not a virgin but a whore, a woman who has willingly corrupted her own innocence before her marriage and at the same time chosen to be unfaithful to the man she loves. In order to prove this accusation, Don John will bring Don Pedro and Claudio below the window of Hero's room on the night before the wedding, where they should hide and watch. On the balcony outside Hero's room, Borachio will make love to Margaret—whom he will have convinced to dress up in Hero's clothing. The watchers will then see a woman who resembles Hero making love with Borachio, and will thus believe Don John's claim that Hero has been false to Claudio. Very pleased with the plan, Don John promises Borachio a large reward if he can pull it off and prevent the planned wedding.

## SUMMARY: ACT II, SCENE III

Meanwhile, ignorant of the evil that Don John stealthily plots, Benedick's friends enact their own benign trick to get Benedick and Beatrice to fall in love. They know that Benedick is currently wandering around in the garden, wondering aloud to himself how, although he knows that love makes men into idiots, any intelligent man can fall in love. He ponders how Claudio can have turned from a plain-speaking, practical soldier into a moony-eyed lover. Benedick thinks it unlikely that he himself will ever become a lover.

Suddenly, Benedick hears Don Pedro, Claudio, and Leonato approaching, and he decides to hide among the trees in the arbor and eavesdrop. Don Pedro and Claudio, noticing him there, confer quietly with each other and decide it's time to put their scheme into effect. They begin to talk loudly, pretending that they have just learned that Beatrice has fallen in love with Benedick. Benedick, hidden in the arbor, asks himself in shock whether this can possibly be true. But Don Pedro, Leonato, and Claudio embellish the story, talking about how passionately Beatrice adores Benedick, and how they are afraid that her passion will drive her insane or spur her to suicide. She dares not tell Benedick, they say, for fear that he would make fun of her for it—since everyone knows what his mocking personality would do. They all agree that Benedick would be a fool to turn her away, for he currently seems unworthy of so fine a woman as Beatrice.

The others go in to have dinner, and the amazed Benedick, emerging from the arbor, plunges himself into profound thought. Don Pedro's plan has worked: Benedick decides that he will "take pity" upon the beautiful, witty, and virtuous Beatrice by loving her in return. He has changed his mind, and far from wanting to remain an eternal bachelor, he now desires to win and marry Beatrice. Beatrice appears, having been sent out to fetch Benedick in to dinner. She deals as scornfully as usual with him, but he treats her with unusual flattery and courtesy. Confused and suspicious, Beatrice mocks him again before departing, but the infatuated Benedick interprets her words as containing hidden messages of love, and he happily runs off to have a portrait made of her so that he can carry it around with him.

---

### Analysis: Act II, scenes ii–iii

Don John's malice resurfaces in Act II, scene ii, as we see him plotting to split Hero and Claudio. Once again, we must wonder about his motives, as his desire to hurt others so badly is inconsistent with his claim to be a low-grade villain. Borachio's statement that his plan, if it succeeds, is sure "to misuse the Prince, to vex Claudio, to undo Hero, and kill Leonato" makes it clear that Don John's schemes have some darker purpose in mind (II.ii.24–25).

In the Renaissance, the virginity of an upper-class woman at the time of her marriage carried a great deal of importance for not only her own reputation but also for that of her family and her prospective husband. Adultery, unchaste behavior, or premarital sex in a noblewoman could be a fighting matter—one that could spur a parent to disown or even kill a daughter, a betrayed husband to murder his wife or rival, or a defender to challenge a woman's accuser to a duel to the death in order to clear her name. If the entire community were to believe Hero unchaste, then her honor, name, and reputation would suffer permanently; Claudio would suffer considerably more than simple vexation; and the stress might well "kill" Leonato. This plot is far more than a merely troublesome game.

Meanwhile, a different kind of trick occurs in the garden, as Leonato, Claudio, and Don Pedro work together to try to convince Benedick that Beatrice is in love with him. Benedick, of course, unknowingly finds himself caught in the position of being the one deceived. He believes that he is eavesdropping upon his friends, but, because they are aware of his presence, they deliberately speak louder so that he will hear them. It is not difficult to imagine the speakers—Leonato, Don Pedro, and Claudio—trying hard to stifle their laughter as they speak in serious voices of Beatrice falling upon her knees, weeping, tearing her hair, and crying, "'O sweet Benedick, God give me patience'" (II.iii.134–135).

Don Pedro understands Benedick's psychology so precisely that his trick works on his friend just as he hoped it would—upon hearing that Beatrice is in love with him and that other people think he will be foolish enough to turn her down, Benedick realizes that it is not so difficult for him to find it in his heart to love Beatrice after all. In a speech memorable for both its humor and its emotional glimpse into Benedick's genuinely generous and compassionate heart, Benedick decides that there is no shame in changing his mind about marriage, and declares, "I will be horribly in love with her. . . . The world must be peopled. When I said I could die a bachelor, I did not think I should live till I were married" (II.iii.207–215).

By the time Beatrice herself appears to order him in to dinner, Benedick is so far gone that he is able to reinterpret all her words and actions as professions of her love for him—doubtless a hilarious scene for the audience, since Beatrice is hostile to Benedick, and the audience knows that she is not at all in love with him. But the buoyant Benedick can hardly wait to "go get her picture"—that is, to go and get a miniature portrait of her (II.iii.232). Later on, Benedick even tries his hand at writing a sonnet to Beatrice. Sonnets and miniature portraits were the typical accoutrements of the Renaissance lover, male or female. By carrying around these objects, Benedick becomes a cliché of Renaissance courtship.

# ACT III, SCENES I–II

## SUMMARY: ACT III, SCENE I

In Leonato's garden, Hero prepares to trick Beatrice into believing that Benedick loves her. With the help of her two waiting women, Margaret and Ursula, she plans to hold a conversation and let Beatrice overhear it—just as Don Pedro, Leonato, and Claudio have done to trick Benedick in the previous scene. Margaret lures Beatrice into the garden, and when Hero and Ursula catch sight of where she is hiding, they begin to talk in loud voices.

Hero tells Ursula that Claudio and Don Pedro have informed her that Benedick is in love with Beatrice. Ursula suggests that Hero tell Beatrice about it, but Hero answers that everybody knows that Beatrice is too full of mockery to listen to any man courting her—Beatrice would merely make fun of both Hero and Benedick and break Benedick's heart with her witticisms. Therefore, she says, it will be better to let poor Benedick waste away silently from love than expose him to Beatrice's scorn. Ursula replies by disagreeing with Hero: Hero must be mistaken, because surely Beatrice is too intelligent and sensitive a woman to reject Benedick. After all, everybody knows that Benedick is one of the cleverest and handsomest men in Italy. Hero agrees, and goes off with Ursula to try on her wedding dress.

After Hero and Ursula leave the garden, winking at each other because they know they have caught Beatrice, Beatrice emerges from her hiding place among the trees. Just as Benedick is shocked earlier, Beatrice cannot believe what she has heard at first. Also, like Benedick, she swiftly realizes that it would not be so difficult to "take pity" on her poor suitor and return his love. She knows how worthy Benedick really is and vows to cast off her scorn and pride in order to love him back.

## SUMMARY: ACT III, SCENE II

Elsewhere, Don Pedro, Claudio, and Leonato begin to tease Benedick about his decision never to marry. Benedick announces that he has changed, and the others agree; they have noticed that he is much quieter. They say that he must be in love and tease him about it. But Benedick is too subdued even to answer their jokes. He takes Leonato aside to speak with him.

As soon as Claudio and Don Pedro are left alone, Don John approaches them. He tells them that he is trying to protect Don

Pedro's reputation and save Claudio from a bad marriage. Hero is a whore, he says, and Claudio should not marry her. The two are shocked, of course, but Don John immediately offers them proof: he tells them to come with him that night to watch outside Hero's window where they will see her making love to somebody else. Claudio, already suspicious and paranoid, resolves that if what he sees tonight does indeed prove Hero's unfaithfulness, he will disgrace her publicly during the wedding ceremony the next day, and Don Pedro vows to assist him. Confused, suspicious, and full of dark thoughts, Claudio and Don Pedro leave with Don John.

---

### ANALYSIS: ACT III, SCENES I–II

The trick that Hero and Ursula play upon Beatrice works just as well as the one Don Pedro and Claudio play upon Benedick in the preceding scene, as Beatrice, just as Benedick does, decides to stop resisting marriage and return her supposed pursuer's love. Clearly, the friends of these two characters know them well. The conversations that Benedick and Beatrice are allowed to overhear are psychologically complicated, appealing to both the characters' compassion and their pride. Beatrice, like Benedick, cannot help but be flattered to hear that her supposed enemy is in fact dying for love of her. But her sensitive side has been targeted: she is disturbed to hear that he is in such distress, and that she herself is the cause. Moreover, it seems likely that her pride is wounded when she hears people say that she has no compassion and that she would mock a man in love instead of pitying him. Just as Benedick is moved to prove the talkers wrong, so Beatrice seems to be stirred to show that she does have compassion and a heart after all. When Hero says, "Therefore let Benedick, like cover'd fire, / Consume away in sighs, waste inwardly. / It were a better death than die with mocks," Beatrice is motivated to "save" poor Benedick and also to show that she is not heartless enough to be as cruel as Hero seems to think she is (III.i.77–79).

Of course, all of these complicated motivations in the friends' plans to dupe Beatrice and Benedick into falling in love with one another relate to the same essential cause: their friends are trying to make Beatrice and Benedick realize that each, in his or her private heart, does have the potential to love the other profoundly. The tricks could hardly work otherwise—Beatrice and Benedick both seem too mature and intelligent to be deluded into thinking that they are in love. Their friends are simply trying to make them realize that they *already* love each other.

Beatrice's speech at the end of the scene is much shorter than Benedick's in the preceding one, but the gist of it is the same. Profoundly affected by what she has heard, she decides to allow herself to change her views about marriage in order to accept Benedick. She has learned how others perceive her—"Stand I condemned for pride and scorn so much?"—and has decided to change these perceptions: "Contempt, farewell; and maiden pride, adieu. / No glory lives behind the back of such" (III.i.109–111). Now, she decides she will accept Benedick if he courts her, "[t]aming my wild heart to thy loving hand" (III.i.113).

In the next scene, however, the atmosphere grows dark. Don Pedro and Claudio's merry teasing of the subdued Benedick amuses, but Don John's shocking accusation against Hero suddenly changes the mood from one of rejoicing to one of foreboding. We also see Don Pedro and Claudio's disturbingly quick acceptance of Don John's word about Hero's unfaithfulness—Don John has promised to show them "proof," but it still seems strange that they so quickly believe evil about Claudio's bride-to-be. Claudio earlier reveals his suspicious nature to the audience when he believes Don John's lie in Act II, scene i that Don Pedro has betrayed him. His susceptibility to suspicion now returns to haunt him, this time with the support and encouragement of Don Pedro.

## ACT III, SCENE III

### SUMMARY

In a street outside Leonato's house, the town policemen of Messina—collectively called the Watch—gather together to discuss their duties for the night. Dogberry, the head constable, and Verges, his deputy, command and govern them. Dogberry and Verges are well intentioned and take their jobs very seriously, but they are also ridiculous. Dogberry is a master of malapropisms, always getting his words just slightly wrong.

Under Dogberry, the Watch is very polite but not very effective at deterring crime. As Dogberry gives his orders to his men, it becomes clear that the Watch is charged with doing very little. For example, when asked how the men should react should someone refuse to stand in Don Pedro's name, Dogberry replies, "Why then take no note of him, but let him go, and presently call the rest of the watch together, and thank God you are rid of a knave" (III.iii.2 5–27). Furthermore, the Watch is supposed to order drunkards to go home and sleep their drunkenness off—unless the drunkards won't listen, in which case the men are to ignore them. The men are not to make too much noise in the street—they may sleep instead. They shouldn't catch thieves, because it isn't good for honest men to have too much to do with dishonest ones, and they should wake up the nurses of crying children—unless the nurses ignore them, in which case they should let the child wake the nurse by crying instead. In short, they may do anything they want and don't have to do anything at all, as long as they are careful not to let the townspeople steal their spears.

Dogberry gives his men a final order: act particularly vigilant near the house of Leonato, for Leonato's daughter, Hero, is to be married the next day, and the house is filled with commotion and chaos. After Dogberry and Verges depart, the men they have left behind sit down quietly on a bench and prepare to go to sleep.

Suddenly, the watchmen are interrupted by the entrance of Don John's associates, Borachio and Conrad. Borachio, who does not see the watchmen, informs Conrad about what has happened this night. Acting on the plan he developed with Don John, Borachio made love to Margaret, Hero's waiting maid, at the window of Hero's room, with Margaret dressed in Hero's clothing. Don Pedro and Claudio, who were hiding nearby with Don John, saw the whole thing and are now convinced that Hero has been disloyal to Claudio. Claudio, feeling heartbroken and betrayed, has vowed to take revenge upon Hero by publicly humiliating her at the wedding ceremony the next day. The watchmen, who have quietly listened to this whole secretive exchange, now reveal themselves and arrest Borachio and Conrade for "lechery," by which they mean treachery. They haul them away to Dogberry and Verges for questioning.

---

## ANALYSIS

Dogberry and Verges provide welcome comic relief amid Don John's evil plotting. Their brand of humor is completely different from that provided by Benedick and Beatrice; while the two witty antagonists spar with a brilliant display of wit, Dogberry and Verges get half their words wrong, providing humor with their ignorance. Yet, like Benedick and Beatrice, they are in their own way good-hearted and sincere, and the humor of both duos, sophisticated and unsophisticated, hinges on punning and verbal display.

Borachio's account of the events of that night inform us that Don John's plans have been put into action and that everything is working out as he intended. Once again, however, we are faced with a disturbing element in this action: Claudio and Don Pedro both believe Don John's claims and are willing to believe that they are watching Hero without investigating the matter more closely or interrogating Hero herself about it. When we see how ready Claudio is to believe that the woman he supposedly is in love with is betraying him, we are likely to be deeply troubled about him, even though we know that the play—being a comedy—has to end happily.

Borachio lists a few factors that might make the deception of Claudio and Don Pedro more understandable. He suggests that we should blame Don John's "oaths," which first made Don Pedro and Claudio suspicious of Hero's guilt; the "dark night, which did deceive them" (III.iii.136–137); and Borachio's own flat-out lies when he testified to them that he had made love to Hero. Some critics focus on the fact that Claudio is quite young and that he does not really know Hero very well as mitigating his distrust of her. Indeed, he seems hardly to have spoken any words to her before they become engaged, although presumably they have conversed more in the week that has passed since their betrothal. Nevertheless, Claudio's swift anger and the terrible revenge he has vowed to take— shaming Hero in public and abandoning her at the altar—has remained troubling to generations of critics and readers, as has Don Pedro's complicity in this desired revenge. Don Pedro, after all, does not have the excuse of youth and inexperience. The brutality of the principal male characters remains a problem with which readers of *Much Ado About Nothing* must grapple. It is difficult to feel sympathy for Claudio and Don Pedro after seeing how quickly they believe evil of Hero—and after what they do to her in Act IV, scene i, on the day of the wedding itself.

## ACT III, SCENES IV–V

### SUMMARY: ACT III, SCENE IV
On the morning of her wedding to Claudio, Hero wakes up early and tells her servant Ursula to wake Beatrice. Meanwhile, Hero's maid Margaret argues affectionately with Hero about what she

ought to wear for her wedding. Hero is excited, but she is also uneasy for reasons she cannot name; she has a strange foreboding of disaster. Beatrice arrives, and Margaret, in high spirits, teases her about her changed personality, saying that now Beatrice too desires a husband. Beatrice expresses annoyance, but Margaret is sure that she is right, and so she continues to tease Beatrice about Benedick—but in a manner subtle enough that Beatrice cannot accuse Margaret of knowing anything completely. Soon enough, Claudio arrives with his friends, accompanied by the large wedding party, apparently ready to take Hero to the church. They all set off together.

## SUMMARY: ACT III, SCENE V

Just as Leonato prepares to enter the church for his daughter's wedding, Dogberry and Verges catch up with Leonato and try to talk to him. They explain that they have caught two criminals and want to interrogate them in front of him. However, their attempts to communicate their message are so long-winded, foolish, and generally mixed up that they fail to convey how urgent the matter is—and, in fact, they may not understand its importance themselves. Leonato defers their business, explaining that he is busy this day, and orders Dogberry and Verges to question the men themselves and tell him about it later. Dogberry and Verges head off to question the prisoners on their own, and Leonato enters the church in order to participate in the wedding ceremony about to take place.

## ANALYSIS: ACT III, SCENES IV–V

The scene in Hero's bedchamber, as Hero prepares for her wedding day, provides an example of some of *Much Ado About Nothing*'s strongest features: the scene combines nonstop jokes with a sense of affection. It means a great deal to Hero to have her cousin and her beloved maids with her on her wedding morning, even amid all the raunchy joking surrounding Hero's impending marriage—for instance, Margaret's statement that Hero's heart will "be heavier soon by the weight of a man" (III.iv.23). Hero's unexpected sense of foreboding sets off warning bells in the minds of the audience. Hero asks God to "give me joy to wear [my wedding dress], for my heart is exceeding heavy" (III.iv.21–22). There is no clear reason for her to feel this way, except perhaps that she must sadly bid her innocent childhood adieu; we interpret her heaviness of heart as a foreshadowing of something bad to come.

Margaret, in high spirits after a night with Borachio, shows remarkable wit in this scene, jesting about Beatrice's conversion to the ways of love. When Beatrice, far more subdued then usual, says that she feels sick, Margaret teasingly offers her a cure—distillation of *carduus benedictus,* or "holy thistle," a plant thought to have medicinal powers in the Renaissance. Beatrice, of course, quite rightly thinks that Margaret is trying to make a point—"Why Benedictus?" she cries. "You have some moral in this Benedictus" (III.iv.10.). Margaret gaily avoids saying concretely what she means, but the gist of the joke is clear: Beatrice is sick with love, and only *benedictus*—that is, Benedick—can cure her. This scene juxtaposes Margaret's dirty punning and overt sexuality with Hero's fearful innocence and utter ignorance of all things carnal. We thus learn how different Hero is from Margaret, and how wrong Claudio is to doubt Hero and mistake Margaret for his untainted beloved.

Act III, scene v, in which Dogberry and Verges try to speak with Leonato outside the church, heightens the tension and our anticipation of an approaching disaster. The two constables entertain us with their foibles as always. In this conversation, Dogberry actually starts pitying Verges and making excuses for his friend's supposed foolishness, although Dogberry himself, as usual, gets many of his words wrong. He calls Verges "an old man," and says, "his wits are not so blunt as, God help, I would desire they were"; he means, of course, "sharp" instead of "blunt" (III.v.9–10). To Verges's response, saying he thinks that he is honest, Dogberry makes the oft-quoted reply, "Comparisons are odorous" (III.v.14). He means to quote the proverb "comparisons are odious." The men that the two constables have caught, of course, are Conrad and Borachio— and Borachio is the one who has helped Don John deceive Claudio and Don Pedro the night before. But because Dogberry and Verges are such poor communicators, they are unable to convey to Leonato how important it is that he hear Borachio's testimony;because they are so foolish, they do not seem to realize how important it is themselves. Thus, Leonato enters the church, and Dogberry and Verges go off without Don John's scheme having been exposed.

# ACT IV, SCENES I–II

*O Hero! What a Hero hadst thou been*
*If half thy outward graces had been placed*
*About thy thoughts and counsels of thy heart!*

(See QUOTATIONS, p. 54)

SUMMARY: ACT IV, SCENE I

Everyone gathers inside the church to celebrate the wedding of Claudio and Hero. But when Friar Francis asks Claudio whether he wishes to marry Hero, Claudio breaks into an outraged speech. He tells Leonato that he sends Hero back to Leonato again, for though she seems outwardly pure and blushes with innocence, her outward features belie her inward corruption and that she is, in fact, an unchaste, unfaithful whore. The happy wedding transforms itself into a chaotic uproar. Leonato and the shaken Hero ask what Claudio means. Claudio tells Leonato, in front of everyone in the church, that the night before Claudio, Don Pedro, and Don John watched Hero "tal[k]" with a vile man at her window (IV.i.82). This man has also "[c]onfessed" to having had sexual encounters with Hero many times before (IV.i.92). Don Pedro supports Claudio's accusations, and they, together with Don John, accuse Hero of sexual looseness. Leonato cries out in despair, asking for a dagger with which to commit suicide. The overwhelmed Hero sinks to the ground, unconscious. Benedick and Beatrice rush to offer her their assistance, while Claudio, Don Pedro, and Don John leave the church without looking back. Leonato, weeping, tells Benedick and Beatrice to let Hero die, since that would be better than for her to live in shame. Beatrice, however, remains absolutely convinced that her cousin has been slandered.

Suddenly and unexpectedly, the friar steps in. A quiet observer to the whole proceeding, he has wisely determined from the expressions of shock he has seen on Hero's face that she is not guilty of unfaithfulness. Hero regains consciousness and insists that she is a virgin, that she has been entirely faithful to Claudio, and that she has no idea what her accusers are talking about. The intelligent Benedick realizes that if the accusation is a lie, it must originate with the troublemaking Don John, who would happily trick these two to spoil their happiness.

The friar comes up with an unexpected plan: he suggests that Hero's existence be concealed, and that Leonato tell everyone she has died of shock and grief. When her accusers hear that an innocent woman has died, their anger will turn into regret, and they will start to remember what a virtuous lady Hero was. If the accusation really is a trick, then perhaps the treachery will expose itself, and Hero can return to the world. In the worst-case scenario, Hero can later be taken off quietly and placed in a convent to become a nun. The grieving, confused Leonato agrees to go along with the plan.

The others depart with Hero, leaving Benedick and Beatrice alone together. Benedick, trying to comfort Beatrice, asks if there is any way he can show his friendship to her. He suddenly confesses that he is in love with her, acknowledging how strange it is for his affections to reverse so suddenly, and she, equally startled and confused, replies in similar terms. But when Benedick says that he will do anything for Beatrice, she asks him to kill his friend Claudio. The shocked Benedick refuses. Angry, Beatrice denounces Claudio's savagery, saying that if she were a man she would kill him herself for his slander of her cousin and the cruelty of his trick. After listening to her, Benedick changes his mind and soberly agrees to challenge Claudio—for the wrong that he has done to Hero and for Beatrice's sake.

### Summary: Act IV, scene ii

Elsewhere, Dogberry, Verges, and the Watch interrogate Borachio and Conrad. Borachio confesses that he received money from Don John for pretending to make love to Hero and then lying about it to Claudio and Don Pedro. When they hear about what has happened at the wedding, the watchmen tie up the captives and take them to Leonato's house.

> *Dost thou not suspect my place?*
> *Dost thou not suspect my years?*
> *O that he were here to write me down an ass!*
> *But masters, remember that I am an ass.*
> (See QUOTATIONS, p. 55)

### Analysis

With the wedding scene—the climax of the play—the tone takes an abrupt turn, plunging from high comedy into tragedy. Claudio's rejection of Hero is designed to inflict as much pain as possible, and Hero's and Leonato's reactions to it seem to make things even worse. Few accusations could cause a woman more harm in the Renaissance

SUMMARY & ANALYSIS

than that of being unchaste, and Claudio uses deliberately theatrical language to hurt Hero publicly, in front of friends and family. The rejection scene also throws other relationships in the play into question: Claudio and Don Pedro both suggest that it reflects badly on Leonato's social manners to have tried to foist off a woman like Hero on Claudio, and Don Pedro implies that his own reputation has suffered by way of the apparent discovery that he and Claudio have made regarding Hero's virginity. Claudio assaults Leonato by denigrating Hero: "Give not this rotten orange to your friend. / She's but the sign and semblance of her honour" (IV.i.30–31).

Although the usually quiet Hero speaks up in her own defense, Claudio does not allow her even the possibility of defending herself. When she blushes in shock and humiliation, he cries:

> . . . Would you not swear,
> All you that see her, that she were a maid,
> By these exterior shows? But she is none.
> She knows the heat of a luxurious bed.
> Her blush is guiltiness, not modesty.
>
> (IV.i.36–40)

Hero's reactions of horror become, in Claudio's description of her face, evidence of her guilt, making it impossible for her to offer any defense. Claudio similarly discards Hero's denial of the accusation when she says, "I talked with no man at that hour, my lord" (IV.i.85). Claudio is convinced—by his eyes, by his own suspicious nature, and by his certainty that he cannot have been mistaken—that he knows the truth. He has already tried and convicted Hero in his mind, and she is afforded no chance to prove her virtue.

Following immediately upon these moments of betrayal and pain, however, seeds are sown for resolution and redemption. The trick that the friar plans is ingenious, and it seems to be a good one. It also plays cunningly upon a simple fact of human nature:

> That what we have, we prize not to the worth
> Whiles we enjoy it, but, being lacked and lost,
> . . .
>
>                          then we find
> The virtue that possession would not show us
> Whiles it was ours.
>
> (IV.i.217–221)

As soon as Hero's accusers think her dead, the friar realizes, much of the anger driving Claudio and the others will dissipate, and they will start to remember her good qualities and regret their poor treatment of her. The "greater birth" that the friar envisions will transform Hero from an object of scorn and slander into someone mourned and better beloved than when she was alive (IV.i.212). In order to wash away her alleged sin, then, Hero will have to die and be symbolically reborn.

The scene also marks a critical turning point in the relationship between Benedick and Beatrice. Benedick seems to make an important decision when he stays behind in the church with Beatrice and her family instead of leaving with Claudio, Don Pedro, and Don John. His loyalty, which lies with his soldier friends when he arrives in Messina, now draws him to stay with Beatrice. In their elliptical ways, Beatrice and Benedick confess their love to one another after everyone else has left the church. Beatrice's confused answer to Benedick's blurting out that he loves her reveals that she is hiding something. Indeed, when Benedick exultantly exclaims that she loves him, she finally admits it: "I love you with so much of my heart that none is left to protest" (IV.i.284–285).

Lost in his newfound love, Benedick apparently converts himself to Beatrice's way of thinking. Soberly he asks her whether she truly believes that Claudio has slandered Hero. When Beatrice answers yes, Benedick says, "Enough, I am engaged, I will challenge him. I will kiss your hand, and so I leave you" (IV.i.325–326). Spurred by his own conscience, his love for Beatrice, and his trust in Beatrice's judgment, Benedick makes the radical decision to challenge Claudio to a duel to the death for what he has done to Hero. The lines of loyalty in the play have changed considerably.

# ACT V, SCENES I–II

## SUMMARY: ACT V, SCENE I

Leonato, Hero's father, falls into a state of deep grief and shock. Torn by his worries about whether Hero is indeed chaste as she claims and his questions about what actually occurred, he cannot function. His brother Antonio tries to cheer him, telling him to have patience. But Leonato answers that although people can easily give advice when they are themselves not unhappy, people in great pain cannot follow the advice so easily. Don Pedro and Claudio enter, see Leonato and Antonio, and quickly try to leave. But Leonato follows them and accuses Claudio of having lied about Hero and having caused her death. Leonato announces that, despite his great age, he challenges Claudio to a duel for the crime Claudio has committed against Hero by ruining her good name; Leonato states that he is not too old to kill or die for honor and for the love of his child. The embarrassed Claudio and Don Pedro pretend to ignore their challengers. Finally, Leonato and Antonio leave, vowing that they will have their revenge.

After Leonato and Antonio depart, Benedick enters. Claudio and Don Pedro welcome him, asking Benedick to employ his famous wit to cheer them up. But Benedick is in no mood to be funny. He tells Claudio that he believes Claudio has slandered Hero, and he quietly challenges him to a duel. When the other two keep on trying to joke with him, Benedick finally discloses that he can no longer be their companion since their slanderous accusations have murdered an innocent woman. Benedick informs Don Pedro that Don John has fled the city and leaves. At first, Claudio and Don Pedro take in this change in Benedick's behavior and the information of Don John's flight with shock and confusion. Slowly they begin to realize Benedick's serious intent—and they rightly guess that his love for Beatrice must be the only thing that could have motivated him to challenge his dearest friend to a fight to the death.

Dogberry and Verges suddenly enter, accompanied by the other men of the Watch, dragging behind them the captured villains Conrad and Borachio. Dogberry tells Claudio and Don Pedro that Borachio has confessed to treachery and lying, and Borachio admits his crime again. Shocked and horrified, Claudio and Don Pedro realize that this information supports Hero's true innocence and that she has died (so they think) because they have wrongly accused her, tarnished her reputation forever, and ruined her family.

Leonato and Antonio return. Claudio and Don Pedro beg Leonato's forgiveness, offering themselves up to any punishment Leonato thinks fit for killing his daughter with wrongful accusations. Leonato orders Claudio to clear Hero's name by telling the entire city that she was innocent and to write her an epitaph—that is, a poem honoring her in death—and to read and sing it at her tomb. He also tells Claudio that Antonio has a daughter who is very much like Hero, and he asks Claudio to marry his niece in Hero's place in order to make up for the lost Hero. Claudio, weeping at Leonato's generosity, accepts these terms. Leonato orders that Borachio be carted away for further interrogation.

### Summary: Act V, scene ii

Meanwhile, near Leonato's estate, Benedick asks Margaret to bring Beatrice to speak to him. Alone, he laments his inability to write poetry. He has unsuccessfully attempted to write Beatrice a love sonnet according to the flowery and ornamental conventions of Renaissance love poetry. Ironically, despite his great skill at improvising in conversation, he is no good at all at writing. Beatrice arrives, and the two lovers flirt and tease each other with gentle insults but also with great affection—as they now seem always to have done. Benedick tells Beatrice he has challenged Claudio to a duel according to her wishes and that Claudio must respond to his challenge soon. Suddenly, the maid Ursula arrives in great haste to tell them that the scheme against Hero has come to light. Benedick pledges his love to Beatrice once again, and the two follow Ursula to Leonato and the rest of the house, which is in an uproar.

### Analysis: Act V, scenes i–ii

By showing Leonato's grief and anger to the audience, Shakespeare drives home the intensity of the pain and distress that Claudio's accusation against Hero has caused Hero and her family. Although Hero is not really dead, Leonato grieves as if she were, because she has lost her reputation. He has come to her side, believing that Claudio must have been wrong about her—"My soul doth tell me Hero is belied," he confesses to Antonio (V.i.42). But his concern for her, coupled with the shock of Claudio's public humiliation of her, is enough to overwhelm him with grief. He rejects Antonio's attempts to make him feel better, telling him that "men / Can counsel and speak comfort to that grief / Which they themselves not feel"

(V.i.20–22). He suggests that once a person actually becomes unhappy, good advice does him or her no good: "For there was never yet philosopher / That could endure the toothache patiently" (V.i.35–36). His anger at Claudio for ruining his daughter is very real, and this scene provides the audience with a fascinating view of Leonato. He is powerful here in his righteous anger, just as much as he is overwhelmed with despair in Act IV, scene i.

The revelation of Borachio's crime to Claudio and the rest marks another turning point in the play. Don John's deception has led inexorably to Claudio's rejection of Hero, darkening the play's atmosphere of lighthearted comedy. Dogberry and the Watch's accusation of Borachio and Conrad seems to open the way to understanding and resolution. Claudio's reaction to the information mirrors what the wise friar predicts in Act IV, scene i: he begins to remember Hero's good qualities. "Sweet Hero, now thy image doth appear / In the rare semblance that I loved it first," he says to himself (V.i.235–236). The punishment that Leonato extracts from him might seem light revenge for the death of a daughter, but, of course, we know—as he knows—that Hero isn't really dead. The punishment obviously establishes the grounds for a happy ending. If all goes well, it seems, Claudio is being set up to marry Hero, in a sort of redemptive masquerade.

Act V, scene ii, which develops the growing relationship between Benedick and Beatrice, is one of the funniest and most touching courtship scenes in Shakespeare's works. It gives the audience a chance to laugh at Benedick and Beatrice as they grapple with the apparent folly of their love for one another, and also to see that their relationship is developing into one that is both affectionate and mature. Moreover, somehow they manage to speak sweetly to each other without losing their biting wit. Benedick, in fact, laughs at himself when he laments his inability to write love poetry. "No," Benedick concludes, "I was not born under a rhyming planet, nor I cannot woo in festival terms" (V.ii.34–35). Benedick's inability to write underlines the difference between the witty and improvisatory court rhetoric that he is so good at and the very stylized conventions of Renaissance love poetry.

Beatrice and Benedick interlace their conversation with news about developments in the main plot of the play, but, throughout, they tease one another with gentle affection—and, of course, with never-ending insults. Benedick sums up their situation by saying, "Thou and I are too wise to woo peaceably" (V.ii.61). This assessment seems to be true in several respects—they will never have peace, for both are too lively and independent. But both are also wise, and it looks as if their love will grow into a deep, mature relationship in which both will continue to sparkle in the other's company. The two also express genuine fondness. To Beatrice's assertion that she feels unwell psychologically, Benedick asks her to "serve God, love me, and mend" (V.ii.78). When she invites him to come with her to talk with Leonato, he answers, "I will live in thy heart, die in thy lap, and be buried in thy eyes. And moreover, I will go with thee to thy uncle's" (V.ii.86–87). Here Benedick plays with a typical Renaissance sexual euphemism, the idea of dying referring to a sexual orgasm.

## ACT V, SCENES III–IV

SUMMARY & ANALYSIS

### SUMMARY: ACT V, SCENE III
Early in the morning, at the tomb where Hero supposedly lies buried, Claudio carries out the first part of the punishment that Leonato has ordered him to perform. Claudio has written an epitaph, or death poem, celebrating Hero's innocence and grieving the slander that (he believes) led to her death. He reads the epitaph out loud and hangs it upon the tomb. He solemnly promises that he will come and read it here at this time every year. Everyone then goes off to prepare for Claudio's wedding to Leonato's niece, the supposed Hero look-alike, which is to occur that very day.

### SUMMARY: ACT V, SCENE IV
Meanwhile, in the church, Leonato, Antonio, Beatrice, Benedick, Hero, Margaret, Ursula, and the friar prepare for the second wedding of Claudio and Hero. We learn from their conversation that Margaret has been interrogated, and that she is innocent of conspiring with Borachio and Don John—she never realized that she was taking part in Don John's treachery. Benedick is also very relieved that Don John's trick has come to light, for now he does not need to fight his friend Claudio. Quietly, Benedick also takes Leonato aside and asks him for his permission to marry Beatrice. Don Pedro and Claudio enter, and Antonio goes off to fetch the masked women. While they are waiting, Don Pedro and Claudio tease Benedick about his love for Beatrice and about the fact that he will soon be married, although they do not know that he actually does plan to be

married that very day. Hero, Beatrice, and the waiting women enter, all wearing masks. Claudio vows to marry the masked woman by his side, whom he believes to be Leonato's mysterious niece. But when Hero takes off her mask, the shocked Claudio realizes that it really is Hero. Leonato and Hero tell him that now that Hero's name has been cleared, she can figuratively come back to life and be his wife, as she should have been before.

The party prepares to go to the chapel to finish the ceremony, but Benedick stops everybody. He asks Beatrice, out loud and in public, whether she loves him. Beatrice denies it, and Benedick, in turn, denies loving her. They both agree that they are good friends, but not in love. But, laughingly, Claudio and Hero tell them that they know that isn't the truth—and both whip out scribbled, half-finished love poems that they have found in their friends' rooms and pockets, written from Benedick to Beatrice and from Beatrice to Benedick. Benedick and Beatrice realize that they have been caught red-handed and, giving in, finally agree to marry. Benedick silences Beatrice, for the first time, by kissing her. Claudio and Don Pedro begin to tease Benedick again, but Benedick laughingly says that he does not care—he remains determined to be married, and nothing he has ever said against marriage in the past makes any difference to him now. He and Claudio assert their friendship again, and Benedick calls for a dance before the double wedding. Suddenly, a messenger rushes in to inform the company that Leonato's men have arrested Don John in his flight from Messina. They have brought him back to Messina a prisoner. Benedick instructs Don Pedro to put off thinking about the villain until tomorrow, when Benedick will invent fine tortures for him. In the meantime, Benedick insists that all must dance joyfully in celebrating the marriages, and he commands the pipers to strike up the music.

───────────

### ANALYSIS: ACT V, SCENES III–IV

This final scene brings the play to a joyous conclusion, drawing it away from the tragedy toward which it had begun to move and letting everyone wind up safe and sound. Claudio and Hero are about to be happily married, as are Benedick and Beatrice. The deception has been revealed, and Don John has been caught and brought to justice. Everybody has made friends again, and the final dance symbolizes the restoration of order and happiness in a world that has been thrown into chaos by Don John's accusation and Don Pedro and Claudio's rash action.

But in order for the play to reach this point, Hero must go through a symbolic death and rebirth, washing away the taint of the accusation of her supposed sin. Claudio's writing and reading of an epitaph at her tomb seems to create a sense of closure, in relation to his false accusation of Hero and her supposed death. He acknowledges his error in having accused Hero: "Done to death by slanderous tongues / Was the Hero that here lies" (V.iii.3–4). The song similarly pleads, "Pardon, goddess of the night, / Those that slew thy virgin knight" (V.iii.12–13). When dawn arrives at the end of the scene, and Don Pedro says, "Good morrow, masters, put your torches out," we can literally see the plot emerging from darkness (V.iii.24). It is now time to attend the wedding meant to release Claudio from his guilt for Hero's death. From darkness and pain, the story now returns to daylight and happiness.

The emotional dynamics of the masked wedding must be complicated, and many readers wonder why Hero still loves Claudio after what he has done to her. The story can be read as one of real love that has been tainted by misunderstanding, paranoia, and fear but that has miraculously ended happily. Hero does seem to love Claudio still, and they are joyful at being reunited. Claudio's amazement, awe, and wonder at finding Hero still alive may serve to wipe out any last traces of resentment or anger on either side.

Beatrice and Benedick finally profess their love in public—amid the laughter and teasing of all their friends—and are clearly happy to be marrying one another. Unlike Hero and Claudio, they are both very communicative people, and there is little doubt as to how they feel about one another. Benedick's long struggle with his aversion to marriage is also finally brought to an end. Just as he privately declares his decision to change his mind after he comes to believe, through Claudio and Don Pedro's trick, that Beatrice loves him, he now announces to the entire world that he is determined to get married, in spite of everything he has said against the institution.

Benedick also renews his friendship with Claudio, and the two of them note with considerable pleasure that they are now relatives. Leonato partakes in this sentiment as well, since Benedick will be Leonato's nephew-in-law. Benedick is so fully changed from a willful cavalier into a submissive lover that he even commands Don Pedro, "Prince, thou art sad, get thee a wife, get thee a wife" (V.iv.117). This order serves partly as a joke, but it contains a drop of melancholy. Perhaps Don Pedro really *is* sad—an idea that seems even more probable when we recall his lighthearted, but perhaps not entirely joking, proposal to Beatrice, in Act II, scene i, and her gentle rejection of it. As so often happens in Shakespeare's comedies, it seems as if somebody must be left out of the circle of happiness and marriage.

At the play's end, Don John is more alienated from the happy company of nobles than he is at the beginning of the play. But Benedick does not even permit us to think about Don John. The villain's torture will take place offstage, after the play's end. The play's closing words are a call to music, and the play's final action is a joyful wedding dance. With the exception of a sad prince and a villain who remains to be punished, everybody has come to a happy ending.

# Important Quotations Explained

1.    The savage bull may, but if ever the sensible Benedick
      bear it, pluck off the bull's horns and set them in my
      forehead, and let me be vilely painted, and in such
      great letters as they write 'Here is good horse to hire'
      let them signify under my sign 'Here you may see
      Benedick, the married man.'

                           (I.i.215–219)

Benedick delivers this speech to Claudio and Don Pedro. Don Pedro
has just quoted an old adage about even the wildest of people eventually calming down enough to submit to love and marriage, suggesting that in time even a savage bull will bear the yoke of a
woman's will. Benedick adamantly refuses to believe this common-
place and decides to mock it. The "sensible" Benedick means the
rational Benedick, a person too intelligent to yield to the irrational
ways of love. Benedick imagines a fantastical scene here, with horns
clapped on his head and writing practically branded into his fore-
head. It was traditional in the Renaissance to imagine that cuck-
olds—men whose wives committed adultery—had horns on their
heads. Benedick's evocation of this image suggests that any woman
he marries is sure to cheat on him. Claudio and Don Pedro continue
to tease Benedick about the bull imagery throughout the play.

2.    What should I do with him—dress him in my apparel
and make him my waiting gentlewoman? He that hath
a beard is more than a youth, and he that hath no
beard is less than a man; and he that is more than a
youth is not for me, and he that is less than a man, I
am not for him.

(II.i.28–32)

These lines constitute Beatrice's witty explanation for why she must
remain an unmarried woman and eventually an old maid: there is no
man who would be a perfect match for her. Those who possess no
facial hair are not manly enough to satisfy her desires, whereas those
who do possess beards are not youthful enough for her. This conun-
drum is not particular to Beatrice. In Renaissance literature and culture, particularly in Shakespeare, youths on the cusp of manhood
are often the most coveted objects of sexual desire.

Although Beatrice jokes that she would dress up a beardless
youth as a woman, there is a hidden double meaning here: in
Shakespeare's time, the actor playing Beatrice would have been
doing exactly that, since all female roles were played by prepubes-
cent boys until the late seventeenth century. Indeed, the beardless
adolescent had a special allure that provoked the desires of both
men and woman on the Elizabethan stage. Beatrice's desire for a
man who is caught between youth and maturity was in fact the sexual ideal at the time. The plot of the play eventually toys with her
paradoxical sentiments for a man both with and without a beard:
during the course of the play, Benedick will shave his beard once he
falls in love with her.

3. They say the lady is fair. 'Tis a truth, I can bear them
witness. And virtuous—'tis so, I cannot reprove it.
And wise, but for loving me. By my troth, it is no
addition to her wit—nor no great argument of her
folly, for I will be horribly in love with her.
(II.iii.204–208)

Benedick has just overheard Claudio, Leonato, and Don Pedro discussing Beatrice's fabricated love for him. Alone on the stage, he
ponders this news and concludes that the best thing for him to do is
to return this love: "for I will be horribly in love with her"
(II.iii.208). This line produces a comical effect, as it seems prepos-
terous that someone would fall "horribly" in love with another person after simply weighing that person's virtues. The choice of the
word "horribly" accentuates the comic aspects of Benedick's decision. Not only does he return her love, but he does so to the point of
overthrowing her, and all others in his midst, with love. The choice
of "horribly" could also echo a bit of the merry war Beatrice and
Benedick have been fighting with their wits. There has always
existed an element of competition between them. It is not enough
for Benedick to reciprocate Beatrice's passions; he must outdo them,
perhaps in order to unseat her and win the competition. The actor
playing Benedick has a number of choices in performing this solilo-
quy: he can reveal that he has always been in love with Beatrice but
is in denial about his true feelings and therefore must go through the
motions of weighing the pros and cons of loving her in a rational
manner. Or he can simply treat this moment as one more parry in
the thrusts and blows of their "merry war" and conclude that the
only way to win is to surpass her, even in love.

QUOTATIONS

4. O Hero! What a Hero hadst thou been
    If half thy outward graces had been placed
    About thy thoughts and counsels of thy heart!
    But fare thee well, most foul, most fair, farewell
    Thou pure impiety and impious purity.
    For thee I'll lock up all the gates of love,
    And on my eyelids shall conjecture hang
    To turn all beauty into thoughts of harm,
    And never shall it more be gracious.
                                    (IV.i.98–106)

Claudio has just openly rebuked Hero at their wedding ceremony, throwing her back to Leonato, her father. He believes that she has not only been unfaithful to him but has lost her virginity, and therefore her purity and innocence, to someone else before her marriage. Claudio's belief is the result of Don John's evil plot to deceive him and make him lose Don Pedro's goodwill. These lines demonstrate Shakespeare's ability to fill a speech with double meanings and wordplay through repetition. For instance, "Hero" appears twice in the first line, changing meaning the second time. The first time, Claudio addresses his former beloved directly. The second time, Claudio compares "Hero" to an ideal conqueror of his heart, as classical heroes conquered and won great battles. Yet Hero has lost her heroic qualities. "Fare thee well most foul, most fair, farewell" plays with repetition and opposites: the sound of the word "fair" is repeated three times in the space of one line, underscoring Claudio's despair at discovering that Hero's outward beauty or fairness conceals a "foul" spirit, as he thinks.

There might also be some play on the double meanings of "fair"—as beautiful, and as balanced and true. In Claudio's eyes, Hero is not only no longer "fair," meaning beautiful (she is "foul"), but she is also no longer "fair," meaning truthful, but is its opposite, false or dissembling. Both the combination of "fair" and "foul" in the same line and "pure impiety and impious purity" in the following line demonstrate a rhetorical technique Shakespeare is famous for using in his plays: *antithesis*, or the combining of paradoxical opposites in one line for emphasis. Moments in which characters spout antitheses usually occur at the height of passion. For Claudio to use these particular opposites to describe his frustration with Hero's seemingly fair exterior and false and foul interior reveals that he is livid with rage and driven to despair.

5.    Dost thou not suspect my place? Dost thou not
      suspect my years? O that he were here to write me
      down an ass! But masters, remember that I am an ass.
      Though it be not written down, yet forget not that I
      am an ass. No, thou villain, thou art full of piety, as
      shall be proved upon thee by good witness. I am a
      wise fellow, and which is more, an officer, and which
      is more, a householder, and which is more, as pretty a
      piece of flesh as any is in Messina, and one that knows
      the law, go to . . . and one that hath two gowns, and
      everything handsome about him. Bring him away. O
      that I had been writ down an ass!

                                    (IV.ii.67–78)

Dogberry is the constable and leader of the town night watch in
Messina, the town where the action of the play takes place. Despite
his comedic substitutions of incorrect words for similar-sounding
correct words, Dogberry does succeed in apprehending Conrad and
Borachio and unraveling Don John's plot to deceive Claudio and
ruin Hero. At this moment, he has caught Borachio and brought
him before the sexton to record the events of the evening. Binding
the villains together, Dogberry calls Conrad a "naughty varlet"
(IV.ii.65). Conrad has angrily responded to Dogberry with "Away,
you are an ass, you are an ass" (IV.ii.66). Dogberry, infuriated that
anyone should insult him, delivers this indignant comic speech filled
with verbal misuse, saying "suspect" instead of "respect" and
"piety" instead of "impiety." Dogberry's determined insistence that
he be "writ down an ass" is comical, because instead of asking that
the sexton note that Conrad has insulted Dogberry, Dogberry con-
tributes to his own slander by insisting that the sexton put in writing
that Dogberry is "an ass." Dogberry is most offended by Conrad's
accusation because the constable interprets Conrad's rudeness as a
class criticism, which it most likely is. Dogberry may not be a nobleman, but he is a good, law-abiding citizen, he owns his own house,
and he possesses two costly pieces of apparel (two gowns), which
signifies that though he does not belong to the court, he is part of the
emergent bourgeoisie. He is right to feel insulted by the ill-behaved
noble Conrad's invective. Though Dogberry's poor command of
the English language results in hilarity, there is nothing poor or evil
about him.

# KEY FACTS

FULL TITLE
*Much Ado About Nothing*

AUTHOR
William Shakespeare

TYPE OF WORK
Drama

GENRE
Comedy

LANGUAGE
English

TIME AND PLACE WRITTEN
1598, England

DATE OF FIRST PUBLICATION
1600

PUBLISHER
Valentine Simmes for Andrew Wise and William Aspley

TONE
Shakespeare's attitude toward courtship and romance combines mature cynicism with an awareness that the social realities surrounding courtship may detract from the fun of romance. The need to marry for social betterment and to ensure inheritance, coupled with the importance of virginal chastity, complicates romantic relationships. Although this play is a comedy ending in multiple marriages and is full of witty dialogue making for many comic moments, it also addresses more serious events, including some that border on tragedy.

SETTING (TIME)
The sixteenth century

SETTING (PLACE)
Messina, Sicily, on and around Governor Leonato's estate

PROTAGONISTS
Claudio, Hero, Beatrice, and Benedick

MAJOR CONFLICT
Don John creates the appearance that Hero is unfaithful to Claudio, and Claudio and Don Pedro come to believe this lie. The real conflict that underlies all of this "ado about nothing" may be that Claudio, Don Pedro, and Benedick share a suspicion of marriage as a trap in which husbands are bound to be controlled and deceived, but they also deeply desire to be married.

RISING ACTION
Claudio falls in love with Hero; Benedick, Don Pedro, and Claudio express their anxieties about marriage in jokes and witty banter; Don Pedro woos Hero on Claudio's behalf; the villainous Don John creates the illusion that Hero is a whore.

CLIMAX
Claudio rejects Hero at the altar, insulting her and accusing her of unchaste behavior; Don Pedro supports Claudio; Benedick, who was most opposed to women and love at the beginning of the play, sides with Hero and his future wife Beatrice.

FALLING ACTION
Benedick challenges Claudio to a duel for slandering Hero; Leonato proclaims publically that Hero died of grief at being falsely accused; Hero's innocence is brought to light by Dogberry; Claudio and Don Pedro repent.

RESOLUTION
By blindly marrying a masked woman whom he believes he has never met, Claudio shows that he has abandoned jealous suspicions and fears of being controlled, and that he is ready to marry. He is rewarded by discovering that his bride is actually Hero.

THEMES
The ideal of social grace; deception as a means to an end; loss of honor; public shaming

MOTIFS
Noting; entertainment; counterfeiting

SYMBOLS

The taming of wild animals; war; Hero's death

FORESHADOWING

Don John's plan to cross Claudio out of jealousy in Act I;
Benedick and Beatrice's witty insults foreshadow their falling
in love.

KEY FACTS

# STUDY QUESTIONS & ESSAY TOPICS

## STUDY QUESTIONS

1.  *Why might it be hard to believe that Hero and Claudio really love each other?*

Many readers have difficulty accepting the romantic relationship between Hero and Claudio. After all, they have barely met before they fall in love and decide to get married, and then Claudio betrays Hero viciously. But the idea of love at first sight was popular in Shakespeare's day. Romeo and Juliet, for instance, fall in love at first sight. Moreover, Claudio's methods of courting Hero through other people would have been an accepted tactic among Elizabethan nobility.

Claudio's belief that Don John's trick is reality is a much bigger problem. Some readers feel that it is impossible to sympathize with Claudio after he rejects Hero in the church. One fact that defends Claudio is that he is young and inexperienced. Also, Don John is very clever—even the older, more experienced Don Pedro is deceived by his ruse. Hero's willingness to forgive Claudio is just as disturbing as Claudio's rejection of Hero. She does not challenge his behavior toward her but instead marries him willingly. In the end, though, Claudio is awestruck and delighted by Hero's unexpected reappearance.

2. *Speech and conversation are important in the play, and many of the characters have distinctive ways of speaking. How do the characters' speech patterns differ?*

The speech patterns of the play's characters vary widely. Some speak with elegance and passion. Two examples of particular eloquence are Leonato's speech after Hero is betrayed and Beatrice's expression of her anger at Claudio. But Benedick and Beatrice also share a special way of speaking all their own, in which they are constantly making jokes and puns; this verbal sparring highlights their special gift of wit. Other characters have no such skill with words. Dogberry is always getting his words wrong to very humorous effect. However, his mistakes hinder communication, as in Act III, scene v, when Dogberry and the Watch try to tell Leonato that they have caught Borachio but cannot make themselves understood. Finally, some characters seldom speak at all, like the sullen and bitter Don John or the gentle but usually shy Hero and Claudio.

3.     *How do gossip, conversation, and overhearing function in the play?*

Much of the plot is moved along by characters eavesdropping on a conversation and either misunderstanding what they overhear or being deceived by gossip or by a trick. Hero, Claudio, and the rest trick Benedick and Beatrice by setting them up to overhear conversations in which their friends deliberately mislead them. Don John's spiteful gossip makes Claudio and Don Pedro suspicious that Hero is disloyal. The window trick, in which Borachio and the disguised Margaret make love at Hero's window, is itself a sort of overhearing. In this case, two people spying on the scene, Claudio and Don Pedro, misunderstand what they see, because Don John has set it up to deceive them. The window scene restages the trick played upon Beatrice and Benedick, but with the opposite effect. Instead of causing two people to fall in love, it causes Claudio to abandon Hero. Finally, at the end of the play, overhearing restores order. The men of the Watch, hearing Borachio brag about his crime to Conrad, arrest him and bring him to justice (III.iii).

4.    *What does the play say about relationships between women and men?*

*Much Ado About Nothing* features one of Shakespeare's most admired and well-loved heroines, Beatrice. Her strength of spirit, sense of independence, and fierce wit place her among the most powerful female characters Shakespeare ever created. But her self-sufficiency does not prevent her from accepting love. Although both she and Benedick have vowed that they will never marry, they change their minds quickly, and both decide that marriage is better than being single. However, Claudio and Hero do not enjoy the strong and egalitarian relationship that Benedick and Beatrice do. Hero's plight reminds us that a woman in the Renaissance was vulnerable to the accusations or bad treatment of men—including her own male relatives. Leonato, in his grief, gives orders to let his daughter die after Claudio abandons her in Act IV, scene i. If not for the intervention of Beatrice and the friar, it is not clear what might have happened to Hero.

# SUGGESTED ESSAY TOPICS

1. *Much Ado About Nothing* is supposedly a comedy: Beatrice and Benedick trade insults for professions of love, and Claudio and Hero fall in love, out of love, and back in love again. But the play contains many darker, more tragic elements than a typical comedy. In what ways is this play tragic?

2. A central theme in the play is trickery or deceit, whether for good or evil purposes. Counterfeiting, or concealing one's true feelings, is part of this theme. Good characters as well as evil ones engage in deceit as they attempt to conceal their feelings: Beatrice and Benedick mask their feelings for one another with bitter insults, Don John spies on Claudio and Hero. Who hides and what is hidden? How does deceit function in the world of the play, and how does it help the play comment on theater in general?

3. Language in *Much Ado About Nothing* often takes the form of brutality and violence. "She speaks poniards, and every word stabs," complains Benedick of Beatrice (II.i.216). Find examples of speech and words representing wounds and battles in the play. What do Shakespeare and his cast of characters accomplish by metaphorically turning words into weapons? What does the proliferation of all this violent language signify in the play and the world outside it?

4. In some ways, Don Pedro is the most elusive character in the play. He never explains his motivations—for wooing Hero for Claudio, for believing Don John's lie, even for setting up Beatrice and Benedick. He also seems to have no romantic interest of his own, though, at the end of the play, without a future wife, he is melancholy. Investigate Don Pedro's character, imagine the different ways in which he could be portrayed, and ascribe to him the motivations that you believe make him act as he does. Why is he so melancholy?

Why does he woo Hero for Claudio? Is he joking when he proposes to Beatrice, or is he sincere? Why would Shakespeare create a character like Don Pedro for his comedy about romantic misunderstandings?

5.  In this play, accusations of unchaste and untrustworthy behavior can be just as damaging to a woman's honor as such behavior itself. Is the same true for the males in the play? How is a man's honor affected by accusations of untrustworthiness or unfaithfulness? Do sexual fidelity and innocence fit into the picture in the same way for men as it does for women? Examine the question of honor and fidelity as it relates to four male characters in the play: Benedick, Leonato, Claudio, and Don Pedro. What could Shakespeare be saying about the difference between male and female honor?

# REVIEW & RESOURCES

## QUIZ

1.  Who refuses to marry in the beginning of the play?

    A.  Hero
    B.  Don Pedro and Don John
    C.  Benedick and Beatrice
    D.  Hero and Claudio

2.  Where and when does the play take place?

    A.  England, fourteenth century
    B.  Florence, fifteenth century
    C.  Sicily, sixteenth century
    D.  Paris, seventeenth century

3.  How does Claudio woo Hero?

    A.  He doesn't; Don Pedro does
    B.  He writes her a sonnet
    C.  He serenades her window at night
    D.  He asks her father to tell her that he loves her

4.  At the beginning of the play, what is Beatrice's relationship to Benedick?

    A.  Lover
    B.  Enemy
    C.  Wife
    D.  Sister-in-law

5.  Who is Leonato?

    A.  Beatrice's father
    B.  Don Pedro and Don John's father
    C.  Claudio's father
    D.  Hero's father

6. What does Don John want?

   A. To marry Hero
   B. To make Beatrice and Benedick fall in love
   C. To ruin Claudio
   D. To kill Dogberry and Verges

7. Who carries out Don John's plan?

   A. Balthasar and Antonio
   B. Dogberry and Verges
   C. Claudio and Don Pedro
   D. Borachio and Margaret

8. What reason does Don John give for his sullenness?

   A. Too many people have wronged him
   B. It's in his nature
   C. It's an act to gain sympathy
   D. He thinks that noblewomen are attracted to brooding types

9. Who is said to be "an ass"?

   A. Dogberry
   B. Borachio
   C. Verges
   D. Conrad

10. Why does Claudio reject Hero at the altar?

    A. She smells like a rotten orange
    B. He thinks she lied to him about her wealth
    C. He thinks she cheated on him and lost her virginity
    D. He decides he just isn't ready to get married

11. Who discovers Don John's evil plot?

    A. Benedick
    B. Margaret
    C. Leonato's household
    D. The Watch

12. What does Leonato's household do to punish Claudio for shaming Hero?

    A.    He pretends Hero is dead and challenges Claudio to a duel

    B.    He drives Claudio out of town

    C.    He violently beats Claudio

    D.    Absolutely nothing at all

13. Which two characters write love sonnets?

    A.    Claudio and Don Pedro

    B.    Claudio and Hero

    C.    Beatrice and Benedick

    D.    Don Pedro and Beatrice

14. To whom does Don Pedro propose marriage?

    A.    Hero

    B.    Ursula

    C.    Beatrice

    D.    Margaret

15. Why is Margaret mistaken for Hero?

    A.    She is wearing a mask

    B.    She is wearing Hero's makeup

    C.    She is wearing a red sash

    D.    She is wearing Hero's clothes

16. Which character is sad at the end of the play?

    A.    Don Pedro

    B.    Don John

    C.    Benedick

    D.    Hero

17. What makes Claudio realize that he wrongly accused Hero?

    A.    A note that she left him

    B.    His utter remorse at having publicly shamed her

    C.    Leonato's harsh reprimands

    D.    Borachio's confession of Don John's plot

REVIEW & RESOURCES

18. When was this play probably first performed?

    A. 1850s
    B. 1580s
    C. 1623
    D. 1599

19. How do Don Pedro and Claudio make Benedick fall in love with Beatrice?

    A. They convince him of her virtues
    B. They have him overhear their conversation in which they assert that she is in love with him
    C. They force him to spend one evening locked in a room alone with her
    D. They insult, humiliate, and belittle him until he agrees to love her

20. Have Beatrice and Benedick courted before?

    A. Yes, but Benedick left her
    B. No, because they're enemies
    C. Yes, but Beatrice left him
    D. They had a blind date when they were younger, but neither of them was interested

21. Why is it necessary for Hero to seem to die?

    A. Because she is very tired and worn out
    B. Because she is pregnant
    C. Because her reputation has been publicly tarnished
    D. Because she cheated on Claudio

22. What term best describes Dogberry's verbal comedy?

    A. Slapstick
    B. Malapropism
    C. Witty banter
    D. Hyperbole

23. What is Balthasar's song in Act II, scene iii about?

    A. The infidelity of men
    B. The infidelity of women
    C. The beauty of love
    D. The wind and the rain

24. What does the "savage bull" symbolize (I.i.213; V.iv.43)?

    A. Happiness in marriage
    B. A world without law
    C. A soldier's honor
    D. The man unwilling to marry

25. Who is the most socially powerful person in the play?

    A. Leonato
    B. Beatrice
    C. Don Pedro
    D. Dogberry

ANSWER KEY:

1: C; 2: C; 3: A; 4: B; 5: D; 6: C; 7: D; 8: B; 9: A; 10: C; 11: D; 12: A; 13: C; 14: C; 15: D; 16: A; 17: D; 18: D; 19: B; 20: D; 21: C; 22: B; 23: A; 24: A; 25: C

# SUGGESTIONS FOR FURTHER READING

COOK, CAROL. "'The Sign and Semblance of Her Honor': Reading Gender Difference in *Much Ado.*" *PMLA* 101 (1986): 186–202.

DAVIS, WALTER, ed. *Twentieth-Century Interpretations of* MUCH ADO ABOUT NOTHING. Englewood Cliffs, New Jersey: Prentice-Hall, 1969.

EVANS, G. BLAKEMORE, et al., eds. *The Riverside Shakespeare.* Boston: Houghton Mifflin, 1974.

GAY, PENNY. "*Much Ado About Nothing*: A King of Merry War." In *As She Likes It: Shakespeare's Unruly Women.* London: Routledge, 1994. 143–177.

GREENBLATT, STEPHEN, gen. ed. *The Norton Shakespeare (Based on the Oxford Edition).* New York and London: W. W. Norton & Co., 1997.

HOWARD, JEAN. "Renaissance Antitheatricality and the Politics of Gender and Rank in *Much Ado About Nothing.*" In *Shakespeare Reproduced,* ed. Jean Howard and Marion O'Connor. New York: Routledge, Chapman and Hall, 1987. 163–187.

# SPARKNOTES
# TEST PREPARATION
# GUIDES

The SparkNotes team figured it was time to cut standardized tests
down to size. We've studied the tests for you, so that SparkNotes
test prep guides are:

## *Smarter:*
Packed with critical-thinking skills and test-
taking strategies that will improve your score.

## *Better:*
Fully up to date, covering all new features of the tests,
with study tips on every type of question.

## *Faster:*
Our books cover exactly what you need to
know for the test. No more, no less.

# SparkNotes Study Guides: